First Steps with SOLO Taxonomy

essential resources

Applying the model in your classroom

Foreword by John Hattie

Pam Hook

Title:	First Steps with SOLO Taxonomy Applying the model in your classroom
Author:	Pam Hook
Editor:	Tanya Tremewan
Designer:	Diane Williams
Book code:	5950
ISBN:	978-1-77655-255-9
Published:	2016
Publisher:	Essential Resources Educational Publishers Limited

United Kingdom:
Units 8–10 Parkside
Shortgate Lane
Laughton BN8 6DG
ph: 0845 3636 147
fax: 0845 3636 148

Australia:
PO Box 906
Strawberry Hills
NSW 2012
ph: 1800 005 068
fax: 1800 981 213

New Zealand:
PO Box 5036
Invercargill
ph: 0800 087 376
fax: 0800 937 825

Websites:	www.essentialresourcesuk.com www.essentialresources.com.au www.essentialresources.co.nz

About the author: Pam Hook is an educational consultant (HookED Educational Consultancy, www.pamhook.com), who works with New Zealand and Australian schools to develop curricula and pedagogies for learning to learn based on SOLO Taxonomy. She has published articles on thinking, learning, e-learning and gifted education, and has written curriculum material for government and business. As well as authoring and co-authoring more than 15 books on SOLO Taxonomy (some of which have been translated into Danish), she is co-author of two science textbooks widely used in New Zealand secondary schools. She is also a popular keynote speaker at conferences.

Acknowledgements: Thanks to Professor John Biggs for his encouragement and ongoing critique of the classroom-based use of SOLO Taxonomy. Thanks to Edendale School (Auckland), Wellesley College (Wellington), and Lincoln High School and St Andrew's College (Christchurch) for providing the photos and examples of student learning outcomes used in this book.

Foreword

In an exciting book on education in the knowledge age, Carl Bereiter (2002) used Popper's (1979) three worlds to make sense of much of what we strive for in school: the physical world, the subjective or mental world, and the world of ideas. These three worlds can be related to the major purposes of schooling: how and what to know about surface knowledge of the physical world, the thinking strategies and deeper understanding of the subjective world, and the ways in which students construct knowledge and reality for themselves as a consequence of this surface and deep thinking. This third world, often forgotten in the passion for teaching facts, is entirely created by humans, is fallible but capable of being improved, and can take on a life of its own. Students often come to lessons with already constructed realities (third worlds), which – if we as teachers do not understand and assess them before we start to teach – can become the stumbling block for future learning. If we are successful, then the students' constructed realities (based on surface and deep knowing) are the major legacy of teaching. It is certainly the case, as Bereiter documents, that "much of what is meant by the shift from an industrial to a knowledge society is that increasing amounts of work are being done on conceptual objects rather than on the physical objects to which they are related" (p 65).

How students think, process, solve problems and increasingly adopt more complex understanding is one of the wonders of our school world. This excitement can easily be dampened by boring learning in rote ways and an emphasis on the facts. On top of this, students can answer too many assessment tasks (in class as well as standardised) by merely knowing lots (despite the psychometricians arguing the item is a deep or complex item). It is much worse when you ask students what it means to learn in class: too often they claim learning is sitting up straight, listening to the teacher, completing the work on time. The love of learning is missing, the thrill and the chase of making connections are lost, and the pleasure of being in the pit of not knowing, working with others to make links and test ideas, is absent.

This conundrum of how to tie together what it is important to know and how we make the connections and extensions to knowing has been tackled by many. The most popular, cited and famous attempt must be Bloom's Taxonomy (Bloom et al 1956). Bloom et al developed a six-level hierarchy of knowledge but it mixes the type of thinking (know, comprehend, apply) with the processing required in completing tasks or answering questions (analyse, synthesise, evaluate). The major problem with Bloom's Taxonomy is that it is largely evidence free – the few evaluations are mainly philosophical treatises noting, among other criticisms, that there is no evidence for the invariance of these stages or for the hierarchy of levels, or arguing that the taxonomy is not based on any known theory of learning or teaching (Calder 1983; Furst 1981). In their review of the evidence for Bloom, Hattie and Purdie (1998) note three major criticisms – namely that Bloom's Taxonomy:

1. presupposes a necessary relationship between the questions asked and the responses to be elicited (see Schrag 1989)

2. separates "knowledge" from the intellectual abilities or process that operate on this "knowledge" (Furst 1981)

3. is not accompanied by criteria for judging the outcome of the activity (Ennis 1985).

In 2001 Bloom's Taxonomy was revised, with the six levels changed to: remembering, understanding, applying, analysing, evaluating and creating (Anderson and Krathwohl 2001). The major change, however, was the addition of another dimension, the complexity of learning, which crosses these six levels of knowing. The complexity of learning itself has four levels: factual – the basic elements of what is needed to know the discipline; conceptual – the interrelationships among these ideas; procedural – how to inquire about these relations; and metacognitive – awareness and knowledge of one's own thinking.

Shortly afterwards, the US-based Common Core adopted a similar taxonomy to the new Bloom levels of complexity, called "depth of knowledge" (Webb 2002). Webb's four levels of complexity are recall; skills and concepts (summarise main idea, solve multiple-step problems, interpret data); strategic thinking (support ideas with examples, develop models, apply a concept in other contexts); and extended thinking (analyse and synthesise information from multiple sources, describe common themes across situations, design models to inform and solve problems).

Despite these attempts to help teachers understand the levels and complexity of knowing, classrooms are still dominated by surface level or "knowing lots". Teachers ask hundreds of questions a day that require simple recall of factual knowledge, much of classroom life is "knowledge telling" and tell and practice, and many tasks can be accomplished by repeating back what the teacher has said. But there can be, and there are, so many successful classrooms where teachers know how to move from surface to deep, from simple to complex. They know where the students are in their current learning and know how to make the next learning more complex. This is where the SOLO Taxonomy comes into its excellence, and there is no better practitioner of this method than Pam Hook.

SOLO Taxonomy stands for the Structure of Observed Learning Outcome Taxonomy (Biggs and Collis 1982, 1989; Collis and Biggs 1986). First developed by analysing the structure of student responses to various tasks in poetry, it has since been applied in almost every school subject. I myself have applied SOLO to evaluating gifted programmes, developing a model of expertise for teachers and coding students' work, as well as in classroom observation schedules and for preparing lesson plans, and it has underpinned nearly all my measurement work (writing and coding items, developing score reports; Hattie and Brown 2004). SOLO Taxonomy consists of a prestructural level plus four levels of learners' performance showing increasing structural complexity: two within surface (unistructural and multistructural), and two within deep (relational and extended abstract). The taxonomy makes it possible, in the course of learning, teaching or assessing a subject, to identify the level at which a student is currently operating. In the simplest language the four SOLO levels showing increasing structural complexity can be named: one idea, multiple ideas, relating the ideas and extending the ideas. That is, one, many, relate and extend.

I have watched others use SOLO in other ways but the best implementer of SOLO is Pam Hook. We first met when she was a renowned teacher of critical thinking programmes and later she helped develop the Gifted Kids programme for Māori and Pacific students. Since then, she has ventured into becoming the best professional developer using SOLO. She has developed materials for schools across many curricula, and has published numerous resources on SOLO. This latest book, *First Steps with SOLO Taxonomy: Applying the model in your classroom*, is another in this excellent series.

This book is one of the best first-start places to not only learn about SOLO but also implement the ways of thinking using SOLO in classes. Pam Hook outlines what SOLO is, where it came from and how it works. She emphasises that SOLO can and should be shared with students, and shows how error (surely we best learn the things we do not know) can be privileged in classes. She shows how to identify effective teaching, learning, e-learning and thinking, and introduces a new language for metacognitive reflection. The sections on applying SOLO in classrooms go beyond the tips and tricks to emphasise the power of SOLO as a way of thinking about planning, teaching, learning and assessing. The section on sharing SOLO with students is a wonderful demonstration of how to teach students to be "assessment capable" and know more about their own complexity of thinking, and helping them know where to go next in their learning.

An important acknowledgement goes to John Biggs and Kevin Collis, who developed this model 25 years ago. John has become a friend to both Pam and myself, and I have researched and published with him on many occasions. His insight, his depth and complexity of knowledge, and his generosity are renowned and much appreciated. I know he has supported Pam in the writing of this book; so please enjoy.

Professor John Hattie
Director, Melbourne Education Research Institute (MERI) and Associate Dean (Research), University of Melbourne

References

Anderson, LW and Krathwohl, DR (eds). (2001). *A Taxonomy for Learning, Teaching, and Assessing: A revision of Bloom's Taxonomy of Educational Objectives.* New York: Longman.

Bereiter, C. (2002). *Education and Mind in the Knowledge Age.* Mahwah, NJ: Erlbaum.

Biggs, JB and Collis, KF. (1982). *Evaluating the Quality of Learning: The SOLO Taxonomy (Structure of the Observed Learning Outcome).* New York: Academic Press.

Biggs, JB and Collis, KF. (1989). Toward a model of school-based curriculum development and assessment using the SOLO taxonomy. *Australian Journal of Education* 33: 151–163.

Bloom, BS, Engelhart, MD, Furst, EJ, Hill, WH and Krathwohl, DR (eds). (1956). *Taxonomy of Educational Objectives: The classification of Educational Goals – Handbook 1 Cognitive Domain.* New York: David McKay.

Calder, JR. (1983). In the cells of Bloom's Taxonomy. *Journal of Curriculum Studies* 15: 291–302.

Collis, KF and Biggs, JB (1986). Using the SOLO taxonomy. *set: Research Information for Teachers* (2): 4.

Ennis, RH. (1985). A logical basis for measuring critical thinking skills. *Educational Leadership* 43(2): 45–48.

Furst, EJ. (1981). Bloom's taxonomy of educational objectives for the cognitive domain: Philosophical and educational issues. *Review of Educational Research* 15: 175–198.

Hattie, JAC and Brown, GTL. (2004). *Cognitive Processes in Assessment Items: SOLO taxonomy* (Tech. Rep. No. 43). Auckland: University of Auckland, Project asTTle.

Hattie, JA and Purdie, N. (1998). The SOLO model: Addressing fundamental measurement issues. In B Dart and G Boulton-Lewis (eds) *Teaching and Learning in Higher Education* (pp 145–176). Melbourne: ACER.

Popper, K. (1979). *Three Worlds.* Ann Arbor: University of Michigan.

Schrag, F. (1989). Are there levels of thinking? *Teachers College Record* 90(4): 529–533.

Webb, NL. (2002). Depth-of-knowledge levels for four content areas. URL: http://facstaff.wcer.wisc.edu/normw/All%20content%20areas%20%20DOK%20levels%2032802.pdf

Contents

Introduction

SOLO Taxonomy is a bit like a watercolour wash. Once the particles of SOLO pigment embed themselves in your mind, you find yourself unable to look at teaching and learning in the same way. Learning is forever visible – viewed through the semi-translucent wash of the SOLO levels.

First Steps with SOLO Taxonomy is designed to help teachers, students and communities use the classroom-based approach to SOLO Taxonomy to make learning in all its guises visible. This accessible, practical book provides a comprehensive overview of SOLO strategies and resources that can be used to create a common language of learning and help students adopt a "growth mindset" about learning and learn to learn. These include strategies that students and teachers can use to *identify* and *describe* what they are doing, *explain* how well it is going and *predict* what they should do next.

The three main sections in this book explore three questions:

- **What is SOLO Taxonomy all about?** Section 1 answers the "frequently asked questions" teachers have about SOLO Taxonomy.

- **Why does SOLO matter?** Section 2 details some of the significant strengths of SOLO that motivate schools to introduce it to teachers and students. It also suggests tasks to help you explore and reflect on your use of SOLO.

- **How can we apply SOLO in the classroom?** Section 3 shows how you can introduce SOLO to the classroom and keep it working in ways that benefit both teaching and learning. It outlines a range of resources for familiarising your students with the model and making it part of your everyday teaching. Also featured are key resources to support you and your students in using SOLO, such as SOLO hexagons and HookED and HOT SOLO maps and self-assessment rubrics.

As you will come to recognise as we move through this book, addressing each of these questions involves a task or an outcome at a different level of SOLO Taxonomy: multistructural, relational and finally extended abstract.

1. What is SOLO Taxonomy all about?

SOLO is a model of learning that makes learning intentions and success criteria visible to students and teachers. With SOLO they have a powerful new language to talk about teaching and learning.

When schools and teachers first nudge up against SOLO, they have many questions. They want to know what the acronym stands for, the evidence supporting the model and how it can be used to improve achievement outcomes. This section introduces SOLO by answering questions teachers commonly ask.

What is SOLO Taxonomy?

SOLO Taxonomy is a model of learning. It is a theory about teaching and learning. SOLO stands for the Structure of the Observed Learning Outcome.

The model represents the increasing structural complexity of learning outcomes as learning progresses through surface, deep and conceptual levels of understanding. It has five distinct levels of learning outcome:

- **prestructural** learning outcomes, where the learner has no idea
- **unistructural** learning outcomes, where the learner has one idea
- **multistructural** learning outcomes, where the learner has several ideas
- **relational** learning outcomes, where the learner has related ideas
- **extended abstract** learning outcomes, where the learner has extended ideas.

The levels represent two changes in the learning outcome: a **quantitative** increase in understanding (knowing more, moving from unistructural to multistructural outcomes) and a **qualitative** change in understanding (deepening of understanding when moving from multistructural to relational to extended abstract outcomes).

In the classroom, you can communicate each of these levels using the terms listed above, or visually through symbols or hand signs, as Table 1.1 illustrates.

Table 1.1: SOLO levels, symbols and hand signs

Prestructural	Unistructural	Multistructural	Relational	Extended abstract
●	▌	▌▌▌	▌▌▌	▌▌▌ ⟳
Learning outcomes show unconnected information and no organisation.	Learning outcomes show simple connections but importance is not noted.	Learning outcomes show connections are made but significance to overall meaning is missing.	Learning outcomes show connections are made and parts are synthesised with the overall meaning.	Learning outcomes go beyond the subject and make links to other concepts – generalising, predicting, evaluating.
No idea	One idea	Many ideas	Related ideas	Extended ideas

Table 1.2 gives examples of verbs that are aligned with each SOLO level. You can use these verbs to indicate what a student would need to be able to do to achieve an outcome at each level (Biggs and Tang 2007).

Table 1.2: Command verbs aligned to SOLO levels

SOLO level	Verbs	Phase
Extended abstract	generalise, predict, evaluate, reflect, create	Qualitative
Relational	sequence, classify, explain, compare, contrast, analyse, relate, apply	
Multistructural	describe, list, outline	Quantitative
Unistructural	define, identify, label, do simple procedure	
Prestructural	*No verbs – student misses the point*	

Where did SOLO come from?

SOLO Taxonomy began as an evidence-based model developed by university academics Biggs and Collis in Australia in the late 1970s. Far from being a "fad" or a "magic bullet", it was developed from extensive research on samples of student thinking. The findings identified their thinking followed a common sequence of increasing structural sophistication in many different subjects (and across many different levels). In his memoir, Biggs (2013) tells the story behind the research.

Another chapter in the story of SOLO began in New Zealand when the Hooked on Thinking Educational Consultancy (now dissolved) developed the classroom-based use of SOLO. It was first introduced to a New Zealand Ministry of Education cluster of primary and secondary schools in 2003. Since then it has been widely used in schools across New Zealand, Australia and the United Kingdom. The classroom-based approach is supported by John Biggs who has acted as a critical friend throughout.

> *I have been through your presentation and again I like it a lot. So by all means you have my permission to proceed as you see fit with that. I trust your judgement in using and interpreting SOLO.*
> John Biggs, personal email communication to Pam Hook

What does SOLO do?

SOLO makes learning visible in any situation where there is a focus on learning. Teachers and students can use it to give proximate, hierarchical and explicit feedback, feed-forward and feed-up on learning.

SOLO makes structure and process visible

Students and teachers can use the model to describe the cognitive complexity of a learning outcome and how learning outcomes change and become more complex as the learner masters an academic task (Biggs 1999). In this way the model provides both:

- a structure for learning – how the ideas are structured (loose, connected or extended ideas)
- a process for learning – what the learning process is (from one idea to several ideas to related ideas to extended ideas).

The focus is on the complexity of the structure of the students' response, rather than on a categorisation of the student themselves. In this way the model allows us to focus on "what the student does" rather than "what the student is" or "what the teacher does" (Biggs and Tang 2007, p 16). The label sticks to the learning outcome not the student, and the conversation is about how the learning outcome can be strengthened or improved, as in this example:

> Your learning outcome for the assignment is at a relational level because you have linked relevant ideas by explaining them using words like "because" and "so that". Your next step is to find more links between the ideas. Perhaps you could think about comparing the event with one that happened in another place or time.

SOLO makes task and outcome visible

We can use SOLO to look at both the learning task and the learning outcome. So, when the task is at one level of SOLO, the outcome can be at another level (emphasising again that the SOLO level relates to the learning outcome, rather than being a label for the individual).

Figure 1.1 gives an example that shows how this separation of task and outcome works. The comparison task is at a relational level because it requires students to have a number of relevant ideas and find similarities and differences to link them. However, a student attempting the task may have an outcome that is:

- unistructural, when they identify one similarity or difference
- multistructural, when they identify several similarities and differences
- relational (like the level of the task), when they can explain the basis for the similarities and differences
- extended abstract, when they can make a generalised claim about the extent or importance of the similarities and differences.

Section 3 introduces some of the range of HOT SOLO and HookED SOLO maps and self-assessment rubrics that support students in undertaking the task and help you and your students to identify the appropriate SOLO level of any learning outcome.

From my experience in schools, teachers and students find it easy to determine:

- what they are doing, based on the SOLO level of the task
- how well it is going, using SOLO-differentiated success criteria
- their next steps, using the "+ 1" strategy of aiming for the next SOLO level.

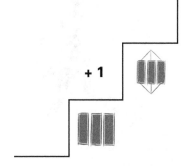

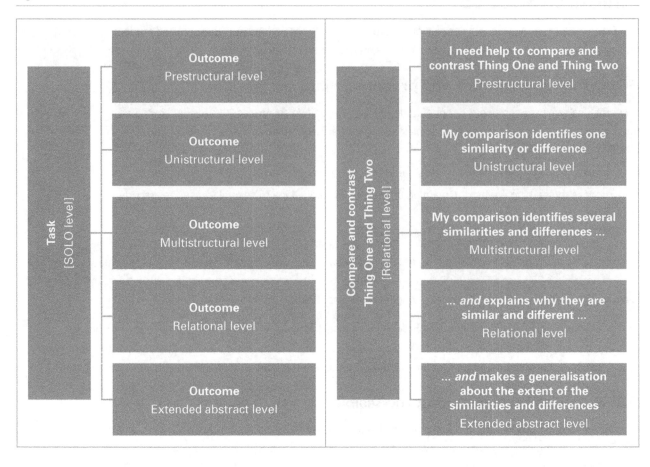

How does SOLO distinguish between declarative and functioning knowledge?

Each of the five SOLO levels describes a learning outcome at a different level of cognitive complexity. You can use these levels to describe outcomes for both:

- functioning knowledge – what students can do
- declarative knowledge – what students know.

Figure 1.2 presents a surfing example to illustrate the difference between these two forms of knowledge.

Figure 1.2: How functioning and declarative knowledge differ

| Functioning knowledge – doing surfing | Declarative knowledge – knowing about surfing |

Differentiating functioning knowledge

Table 1.3 shows how SOLO differentiates functioning knowledge based on its five levels of learning outcomes.

Table 1.3: Success criteria for a SOLO functioning knowledge task

Prestructural	Unistructural	Multistructural	Relational	Extended abstract
No performance outcome	Performance outcome based on following instructions or modelling the actions of another	Independent performance outcome without understanding why or when; makes mistakes	Independent performance outcome based on informed decision-making; can correct mistakes	Independent performance outcome that extends existing performance in new ways

The different levels of functioning knowledge outcomes are evident:

- when students are asked to apply their understanding in a particular setting – for example, when determining the pH of a solution or turning a kayak with a forward sweep stroke
- through competencies and capabilities for living and learning with others – for example, when reflecting, managing self, behaving ethically, demonstrating a "can do" attitude or looking out for others.

The generic self-assessment rubric for functioning knowledge in Table 1.4 has been built using SOLO Taxonomy. You can generate your own rubric for a specific task with the online HookED Functioning Knowledge Rubric Generator: http://pamhook.com/solo-apps/functioning-knowledge-rubric-generator

Table 1.4: SOLO self-assessment rubric for functioning knowledge

Functioning knowledge	Prestructural	Unistructural	Multistructural	Relational	Extended abstract
Outcome	[needs help]	[if directed]	[aware but no reasons, has a go, makes mistakes]	[purposeful, strategic, knows why and when, can identify mistakes]	[new ways, seeks feedback to improve, acts as role model, teaches others]
Learning intention [verb] [content] [context]	I need help to start.	I can [xxxx] if directed or shown exactly what to do.	I can [xxxx] but I don't know why or when so it is trial and error. I make mistakes.	I can [xxxx] and I know why and when. I am strategic or purposeful and can find and correct my own mistakes.	I can [xxxx] and I know why and when. I seek feedback to improve what I am doing. I help others. I am a role model for others. I find new ways of doing [xxxx].

Differentiating declarative knowledge

SOLO differentiates declarative knowledge according to what students can write about or talk about in different contexts. A student's learning outcome is evident in their response to a task in which they are to describe what they know about a particular topic, character or theme, such as citizenship and democracy, carbon footprints and climate change, changes in the transport infrastructure of big cities, nutritional needs of elite athletes or bullying through social media.

Table 1.5 sets out a generic self-assessment rubric for declarative knowledge built from SOLO levels. You can generate your own rubric for a specific task with the online HookED Declarative Knowledge Rubric Generator: http://pamhook.com/solo-apps/declarative-knowledge-rubric-generator

Table 1.5: SOLO self-assessment rubric for declarative knowledge

Declarative knowledge	Prestructural	Unistructural	Multistructural	Relational	Extended abstract
Outcome	[needs help]	[one relevant idea]	[several relevant ideas]	[linked ideas]	[extended ideas]
Learning intention [verb] [content] [context]	I need help to start.	My [learning outcome] has one relevant idea.	My [learning outcome] has several relevant ideas.	My [learning outcome] has several relevant ideas and links these ideas. *(Verbs for linking – sequence, classify, compare and contrast, explain causes, explain effects, analyse part–whole)*	My [learning outcome] has several relevant ideas, links these ideas and looks at them in a new way. *(Verbs for looking in new ways – generalise, evaluate, predict, create)*

Example: What did you learn from reading the article about the food we eat? The following are examples of students' declarative knowledge responses to this question at each level of SOLO Taxonomy. As noted above, the progression from prestructural to multistructural outcomes is quantitative (bringing in information) whereas the progression from multistructural to relational and extended abstract outcomes is qualitative.

- **Prestructural:** The student tackles the task inappropriately, has missed the point, needs help to start or simply restates the question:

    We eat food.

- **Unistructural:** The student picks up one aspect of the task and their understanding is disconnected and limited:

    The food we eat comes from plants or animals.

- **Multistructural:** The student knows several aspects of the task but misses their relationships to each other and the whole:

    The food we eat comes from plants or animals. These plants and animals are mostly raised on farms or grown in gardens. It can take some time before the plants and animals are ready to eat. Farmers and horticulturists commonly use tools and machines to help them plant, grow and harvest the plants and animals. Different cultures often have different customs about the type of food they eat and how that food is prepared.

- **Relational:** The student links and integrates the aspects of the task, which contributes to a deeper level of understanding – and a more coherent understanding of the whole:

    The food we eat comes from plants and animals **because** they are a source of the essential nutrients required for our life and health. These plants and animals are mostly raised on farms or grown in gardens **because** agriculture allows a more efficient food supply with increased yields to better meet the needs of large populations than hunting and gathering. It can take some time before the plants and animals are ready to eat **because** it takes a long time to grow a seed into a mature wheat plant before it can be harvested, processed, changed into a loaf of bread and transported to a supermarket. Similarly it takes a long time to produce and raise calves to beef cattle, to transport them to a processing plant and from there to a packing house where the meat patties are created and distributed to food outlets so that the hamburger can be sold at a takeaway food outlet. Farmers and horticulturists use tools and machines to help them plant, grow and harvest the plants and animals **so that** they can be more productive. This is **because** the tools take less work (energy) to operate than doing the same job by hand. Different cultures often have different customs about the type of food they eat and how that food is prepared **because** climate and other features of the place in which you live influence the foods that can grow there.

- **Extended abstract:** Taking their new understanding at the relational level, the student rethinks it at another conceptual level, looks at it in a new way and uses it as the basis for prediction, generalisation, reflection or creation of new understanding:

  The food we eat comes from plants and animals because they are a source of the essential nutrients required for our life and health. These plants and animals are mostly raised on farms or grown in gardens because agriculture allows a more efficient food supply with increased yields to better meet the needs of large populations than hunting and gathering. It can take some time before the plants and animals are ready to eat because it takes a long time to grow a seed into a mature wheat plant before it can be harvested, processed, changed into a loaf of bread and transported to a supermarket. Similarly it takes a long time to produce and raise calves to beef cattle, to transport them to a processing plant and from there to a packing house where the meat patties are created and distributed to food outlets so that the hamburger can be sold at a takeaway food outlet. Farmers and horticulturists use tools and machines to help them plant, grow, harvest, transport and process the plants and animals so that they can be more productive. This is because the tools take less work (energy) to operate than doing the same job by hand. Different cultures often have different customs about the type of food they eat and how that food is prepared because climate and other features of the place in which you live influence the foods that can grow there.

  After reading the article I think the foods we eat in the future will be very different from what we eat today. This is **because** new technologies in food production and processing and a greater concern for the impact of what we choose to eat on energy use on planet Earth will see us eating more unprocessed foods, more plants and less meat. **My evidence for this claim is** that we can already see increasing numbers of young people choosing to eat for the health of the planet rather than eating to belong to a particular culture or family tradition.

What does SOLO assume?

The SOLO model assumes that, as learning progresses, the student's responses change. Hattie and Brown (2004) describe this as a shift:

- from concrete understanding to abstract understanding
- from low demand on working memory to high demand on working memory
- from a greater need for closure (than consistency) to a greater need for consistency (than closure) and then to an accommodation of inconsistency
- from thinking in terms of a single relationship, to multiple relationships, to integrated relationships and to extending these relationships to some place new, beyond the original context.

As learning progresses, we can use these changes in a student's response to help us make good decisions about the teaching strategies we should adopt. As Table 1.6 identifies, the most appropriate strategies will change as there is a shift in the demand on working memory and the balance of need for closure or consistency.

Table 1.6: Effective teaching strategies at different levels of SOLO learning outcome

	Demand on working memory	Need for closure and consistency	What the learner does	What the teacher does
Prestructural	Not applicable	Not applicable	Is unable to make a claim or makes an unrelated claim	Teaches for engagement
Unistructural	Surface understanding Low demand on working memory [recall strategies]	High need for closure and lower need for consistency *For example, attempts to complete the task with minimal effort*	Makes a claim in relation to one aspect	Teaches for automaticity of content and skills through learning, modelling, repetition and practice
Multistructural		Moderate need for closure and consistency *For example, uses isolated facts or independent ideas in an attempt to get the task out of the way*	Makes a claim in relation to several independent aspects	Teaches for increasing and consolidating content and skills through learning, repetition and practice
Relational	Deep and conceptual understanding High demand on working memory [relating and transforming strategies]	High need for consistency and can delay the need for closure *For example, seeks out clearly accessible new knowledge to improve the coherence of their understanding*	Makes a claim integrating ideas in relation to a given or experienced context	Teaches for interrelationships – the integration of content and skills within an organising principle
Extended abstract		Is prepared to accommodate inconsistency *For example, is prepared to defer conclusions to accommodate reflection, hypothesising or paradox*	Makes a claim in relation to a context not yet experienced (or beyond the original context)	Teaches for abstract concepts or relationships that sit outside the original organising principle

When we use SOLO to make learning visible (as in Table 1.2 above), we can also determine students' prior knowledge and, from this information, identify the most effective teaching strategies and approaches to help them make progress in their learning. For example, teaching for engagement is useful when students know very little about the ideas being taught but teaching for relatedness – helping students make links between what they know and an organising principle – will be more valuable when they have consolidated content knowledge and skills about an idea.

Which learning areas and age groups does SOLO apply to?

SOLO is a generic model. It can be used to categorise any learning outcome (functioning or declarative knowledge) in any learning area on the basis of its cognitive complexity.

Moreover, given its simplicity in conceptualising learning as moving from loose ideas to connected ideas to extended ideas, the taxonomy can be used reliably with and by learners of all ages. Learners may benefit whether they are five-year-olds just starting school or 85-year-olds learning how to use social media.

Do teachers and students agree about the SOLO level of a learning outcome?

In my experience, given the simplicity of the model, it is easy for people to agree on the SOLO level of a given learning outcome. Teachers and students, and students among themselves, tend to agree on the SOLO level in discussions about students' learning outcomes. Similarly, different teachers tend to allocate the same SOLO level to a given learning outcome: Hattie and Brown (2004, p 17) have found the model has high levels of teacher inter-rater reliability.

Where can I find out more about SOLO?

Start with:

1. J Biggs and C Tang. (2007). *Teaching for Quality Learning at University. What the student does*
2. P Hook. (2013). *A Children's Guide to SOLO Taxonomy: Five easy steps to deep learning.*

Follow up with any of the SOLO titles on classroom-based practice on the Essential Resources website (see the front of this book for details on the site in your region).

For updates on classroom-based practice, keep an eye on:

- SOLO Taxonomy on Pinterest boards: **www.pinterest.com/solotaxonomy**
- SOLO Taxonomy blog posts: **www.diigo.com/list/artichoke/SOLO+Taxonomy+Blogs/1xnsxfo84**
- SOLO on Twitter: #solotaxonomy
- Pam Hook on Twitter @arti_choke
- SOLO Taxonomy on YouTube: **www.youtube.com/user/Chokearti**

2. Why does sharing SOLO with students matter?

As a profession we do not ask enough "whys". Anytime we are asked to adopt something new we should ask "serial whys". Why SOLO? Why share the model? Why a common language? Why make learning visible? Why a growth mindset? It seems that SOLO can stand the interrogation.

SOLO is a sandbox model – a flexible and adaptable model of learning. Much like a sandbox, it can be used in many different ways for many different purposes in teaching and learning, such as for supporting effective strategies and interventions in planning, teaching, feedback and assessment. This section elaborates on why using SOLO with students in the classroom matters.

The following are 16 solid reasons why schools share SOLO with students and teachers.

Learning is all about effort and effective strategies

Dweck's (1999, 2006) work on motivation and students' mindset reveals that when a student believes their learning outcome is due to luck or fixed ability (high or low), it puts them at risk. They give up on tasks early and fail to challenge themselves to do better, instead seeking easier tasks where they feel less likely to fail or more likely to achieve (see Mangels et al 2006).

A powerful outcome of using SOLO is that the model confronts the self-limiting mindsets about learning that many students hold. By making the structure of the learning outcome visible to students, SOLO emphasises that they achieved a particular outcome because they used effort and strategies to pull in ideas, connect ideas or extend ideas in new ways. For example, their relational learning outcome is not due to luck or fixed ability – it is due to their effort in looking for similarities and differences between ideas and their use of the comparison thinking template to help organise their ideas.

Task: Google "growth mindset", a simple idea based on the research of Stanford University psychologist Carol Dweck. Read the research behind the idea. Listen to the way you and your colleagues talk about students and their learning. When do you notice "fixed mindset" conversations occurring? Reframe these conversations so that they portray a growth mindset.

Re-positioning "knowing nothing" and "needing help to start"

Peer pressure and social norms can make students reluctant to acknowledge they know little about a topic and ask for help to start. SOLO positions "knowing nothing" (having a prestructural learning outcome) as a necessary step to any adventure in learning. Everyone, no matter what their background is, will find themselves with a prestructural learning outcome at some point when learning. When they do, the SOLO model shows that knowing nothing is a common starting point for many learners and gives students a clear idea about what to do next. In seeking to shift their learning outcome from prestructural to unistructural, students can work to bring in one relevant idea or model the performance outcomes of another student already at the unistructural level.

Task: Reflect on a time in your life when you struggled to make sense of a conversation or direction and chose to fake understanding rather than ask for clarification. What prevented you from saying that you did not understand? Can you think of a contrasting experience when you felt comfortable telling others you did not understand? How can you use SOLO to create a similar high-trust environment for students in your classroom?

Mistakes, errors and "not knowing" are opportunities to learn

Environments where powerful learning happens are defined by errors and mistakes. However, for social and other reasons, students may work to disguise their errors and misunderstanding and thus self limit and/or distance themselves from opportunities to learn.

SOLO identifies that errors and "not knowing" are indicators that learning is happening. When they use SOLO as a model of learning, students can see that having a go and making errors (multistructural outcome) is a deeper learning outcome than waiting for direction, prompting or modelling from others (unistructural outcome).

Task: While observing classrooms, including your own, monitor the times when "errors" are framed as opportunities for new learning. Challenge yourself and your colleagues to actively embrace errors as indicators of and prompts for new learning.

Making visible the gap between what students know and the desired learning goal

By making visible the structure of the existing and the desired learning outcome, students can construct next steps in learning through goal setting and targeting to shift the SOLO level of their outcome towards the desired learning goal (Figure 2.1 and Table 2.1).

Figure 2.1: Using "next steps" to reach the desired learning goal

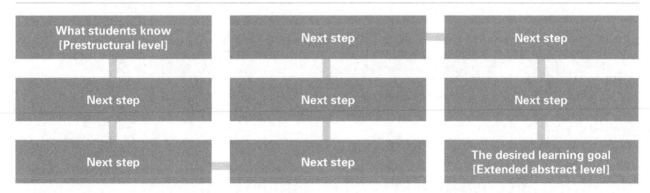

Table 2.1: Making the gap visible between where I am now and where I want to be

Where I am now	Activities that will help me close the gap	Where I want to be – desired learning outcome
I have described three driver distractions when operating a vehicle. This is a multistructural outcome – the structure of my response shows loose ideas.	**Explain how** the distraction affects the driver. (Relational task) **Explain why** the distraction puts the driver and others sharing the same road at risk. (Relational task) **Generate** potential solutions to the driver distractions. (Extended abstract task) **Evaluate** potential solutions to the driver distractions. (Extended abstract task)	I want to plan and implement solutions to help drivers manage distractions when driving. This is an extended abstract outcome – the structure shows ideas are being connected and then extended in new ways.

Task: Complete a table like Table 2.1 above in which you describe the gap between "what your students know" about something and "what you would like them to know". Detail the learning experience that will help close the gap. Share your gap-closing activities with a colleague. What activities do they suggest will close the gap? Allocate a SOLO level to each of the tasks identified.

Identifying effective teaching and learning approaches to reach a learning goal

By identifying the cognitive load students experience when thinking at different levels of SOLO – when bringing in ideas, connecting ideas and extending ideas – SOLO provides a rationale for what teachers might do. It helps us understand why some teaching approaches will be more effective than others at different stages of helping students reach a learning goal.

When students have:

- a prestructural understanding of the content, we should **teach for engagement**
- a unistructural understanding of the content and a high need for closure over consistency, we should **teach for automaticity of content and skills** through learning, modelling, repetition and practice
- a multistructural understanding of the content and a moderate need for closure and consistency, we should **teach for increasing and consolidating content and skills** through learning, repetition and practice
- a relational understanding of the content and a high need for consistency such that they can delay closure, we should **teach for interrelationships**, integrating content and skills within an organising principle
- an extended abstract understanding of the content, we should **teach for abstract concepts** or relationships that sit outside the original organising principle.

See also Table 1.6 in Section 1.

Task

1. Hold a professional learning session with teachers in your team, syndicate or department. Ask teachers to work in pairs to share and develop teaching strategies and approaches suitable for each SOLO level above. For example, ask, "How will you teach for engagement? How will you teach for interrelationships?"

2. Develop a visual analogy or metaphor for SOLO. Play with the thinking around loose ideas, connected ideas and extended ideas. Share your visual metaphors on a board in the staff workroom.

Identifying effective thinking and e-learning strategies to reach a learning goal

Although thinking skills and e-learning strategies are often used in the classroom, they may be used more purposefully when they are coded in ways that help students reach their desired learning goals. That is, they can be coded as:

- strategies that help students bring in and remember loose ideas
- strategies that help students link or integrate ideas under some organising principle
- strategies that help students extend these ideas to abstract concepts or relationships that sit outside the original organising principle.

From there, teachers and students can create thinking and e-learning strategy toolboxes where different strategies are categorised in terms of their purpose. For example, if the learning task involved linking ideas (relational level), then the student could select from a range of thinking strategies that support tasks at this level (see Table 2.2 for examples).

Table 2.2: A toolbox of strategies for a task involving comparison (relational level)

Relational task	Thinking strategies to support task
Comparison – linking ideas by finding similarities and differences	Venn diagram, double bubble map, de Bono plus–minus–interesting, compare and contrast writing template etc

By using SOLO levels to align learning strategies and supports (thinking strategies and e-learning tools) with learning experiences, teachers can add choice and challenge to student learning (Table 2.3). Even when strategies can be used across all levels of SOLO outcome – for bringing in ideas, linking ideas or extending ideas – identifying how the e-learning tool is being used in this instance brings purpose to students' efforts.

Table 2.3: Examples of thinking strategies and e-learning differentiated against SOLO levels

Unistructural	Multistructural	Relational	Extended abstract
Strategies for bringing in ideas		Strategies for connecting ideas	Strategies for extending ideas
HOT SOLO Define map and self-assessment rubric De Bono Red Hat thinking Google "Define" strategy (type "Define" in front of a word in Google search to access its definition)	HookED SOLO hexagons HOT SOLO Describe map and self-assessment rubric De Bono White Hat thinking Brainstorming Instagrok: **www.instagrok.com**	HookED SOLO hexagons HOT SOLO Sequence, Classify, Compare and contrast, and Analyse maps and self-assessment rubrics HookED SOLO Explain causes, Explain effects, and Make an analogy maps and self-assessment rubrics De Bono Yellow Hat and Black Hat thinking De Bono CoRT plus–minus–interesting routine Explain Everything app: **www.morriscooke.com/?p=134**	HookED SOLO hexagons HOT SOLO Generalise, Predict and Evaluate maps and self-assessment rubrics HookED SOLO Describe++ map and self-assessment rubric de Bono Blue Hat and Green Hat thinking "What if" questions Rationale: **http://rationale.austhink.com** Values Exchange all schools project: **www.vxcommunity.com**

Task

1. Hold a staff meeting where teachers bring examples of the thinking skills and strategies they commonly use with students. In small groups, they think about the learning purpose of each strategy. Is it a strategy that is great for connecting ideas – like Ishikawa's fishbone diagram for causal thinking – or that can be use in different ways to help bring in ideas, connect ideas and extend ideas like SOLO hexagons or the "See Think Wonder" routine? Contribute the ideas to a collaborative document as a school-wide thinking strategy resource.

2. Work with students across the year to build a class toolbox of thinking and e-learning strategies for reaching learning goals at different levels of cognitive complexity according to SOLO. Encourage students to "like" or "up vote" strategies as being more or less useful and to build their own SOLO strategy toolboxes.

Assessing both functioning and declarative knowledge outcomes

A versatile model, SOLO can be used to measure students' performance when they are:

- learning about things – declarative knowledge (DK)
- learning to do things – functioning knowledge (FK).

This versatility is useful in a profession like teaching where both functioning and declarative knowledge outcomes are sought in every learning area. For example, one of these two outcomes is sought when learning to: use punctuation (FK), paddle a kayak (FK), use language to describe a character (DK), write a persuasive blog post (DK) or give an oral presentation (FK) on the analysis of a student survey (DK). (See also Tables 3.1, 3.4 and 3.5 in Section 3.)

A generic measure of learning outcomes across subjects and levels

SOLO is applicable across all content, curriculum levels and ages. It can be used to measure the complexity of a learning outcome in different subjects and disciplines and within different learning environments. It can also be used with different curriculum levels and with different ages of students.

For example, teachers and students can use SOLO when:

- thinking like a mathematician (Table 2.4)
- thinking like a visual artist (Table 2.5)
- preparing a campsite on an outdoor education overnight camp (Table 2.6)
- comparing and contrasting an earthquake and a volcano (Table 2.7).

Table 2.4: SOLO self-assessment rubric when working mathematically (functioning knowledge)

Working mathematically	Prestructural	Unistructural	Multistructural	Relational	Extended abstract
	I struggle to make sense of all the information. I don't know how to start. I guess.	I can find one piece of information or heuristic that seems familiar and work on that.	I can use more than one piece of information in the problem but I cannot work out how they all connect to form a workable solution to the whole problem.	I can integrate my different calculations, measurements or drawings to form a workable solution to the problem and give a logical explanation for each step.	I can generalise the integrated solution, introduce new elements, modify the solution and apply the solution to novel situations.
	My solution simply restates the problem.	My solution identifies one relevant piece of information and uses it in a calculation, measurement or drawing.	My solution identifies several relevant pieces of information and uses them in calculations, measurements or drawings without offering any justification for my actions.	My solution identifies several relevant pieces of information and uses them in calculations, measurements or drawings. I justify my actions (in diagrams and words) deduced from the nature of the problem.	My solution extends these justifications, making generalisations, abstractions and exceptions to include/ integrate other variables and contexts.
Effective strategies *[insert strategies suggested by students and teachers]*	Show examples. Give opportunity to practise.	Give clear instructions (step by step). Prompt. Do situational teaching.	Revisit, recap and remind.	Give repeated opportunities to practise.	

Table 2.5: SOLO self-assessment rubric for the visual arts (functioning knowledge)

Visual arts	Prestructural	Unistructural	Multistructural	Relational	Extended abstract
Note: Content and context determine the level	I gather information but it is often not relevant to the task.	I gather relevant information if directed or prompted.	I gather relevant information in a range of different formats ...	... **and** I can justify the relevance of the information I gather ...	... **and** I explore the conceptual understandings, insights and essential questions raised by the information I gather.
	I need help to use the information I gather.	I use the information I gather to help me come up with a possible solution to the task.	I use the information I gather to come up with many diverse solutions from different perspectives ...	... **and** I am strategic and purposeful when interpreting the relevant information. I think about how the elements, processes and procedures can be integrated to make meaning in my artwork.	I integrate the elements, processes and procedures to meet the challenge of the brief.
	I need help to come up with a solution to the task.	I draw on existing solutions for my ideas.	I see making art as a process of interpreting ideas to develop solutions.	I see making art as an act of communicating a message to different audiences.	I see making art as a way of developing a personal world view.
	I need help to engage with the task of making art.	I engage with the task of making art if prompted or directed.	I engage with the task but I am not sure why or when to use the different elements, processes and procedures.	I engage with the task of making art. I can recognise professional standards when making art.	I engage with making art as part of a wider community of artists.
Effective strategies [insert strategies suggested by students and teachers]	Show examples. Give opportunity to practise.	Give clear instructions (step by step). Prompt. Do situational teaching.	Revisit, recap and remind.	Give repeated opportunities to practise.	

Table 2.6: SOLO self-assessment rubric for setting up camp for a camping experience (functioning knowledge)

Setting up camp	Prestructural	Unistructural	Multistructural	Relational	Extended abstract
Factors to consider include vegetation, contour of land, weather, environmental hazards, safe group movement, proximity to water, land managers, local hapū, communal living (toilets, cooking, waste, water, food, personal washing)	I need help to set up camp.	I can set up camp if I am prompted or directed.	I use several strategies to set up camp but I am not sure when and/or why to use them. *(Trial and error – aware of strategies but not sure why or when to use them so makes mistakes)*	I use several strategies to set up camp and I know when and why to use them. *(Strategic or purposeful use of strategies – knows why and when)*	I can teach others to set up camp. I act as a role model for others to help them set up camp. I seek feedback on how to improve how I set up camp.
Effective strategies [insert strategies suggested by students and teachers]	Show examples. Give opportunity to practise.	Give clear instructions (step by step). Prompt. Do situational teaching.	Revisit, recap and remind.	Give repeated opportunities to practise.	

Table 2.7: SOLO self-assessment rubric for comparing an earthquake and volcanic eruption (declarative knowledge)

Compare and contrast an earthquake and volcanic eruption	Prestructural	Unistructural	Multistructural	Relational	Extended abstract
	I need help to compare and contrast an earthquake and a volcanic eruption.	My comparison has one relevant similarity or difference.	My comparison has several relevant similarities and differences …	… **and** I can explain these similarities and differences …	… **and** I can make a generalisation about the similarities and differences.
Effective strategies [insert strategies suggested by students and teachers]					

Task

1. Construct a SOLO rubric for describing the attributes of a character in a narrative. The rubric should be suitable for use by primary school students describing a character in a picture book and by secondary school students describing a character in a novel study. Use text or annotated images to explain the success criteria at each level. Go online for the HookED SOLO Declarative Knowledge Rubric Generator: **http://pamhook.com/solo-apps/declarative-knowledge-rubric-generator**

2. Construct a SOLO rubric for measuring. The rubric should be suitable for use by primary school students learning to measure length with a ruler and older students measuring angles with a protractor or the height of a building with a hand-held range finder. Go online for the HookED SOLO Functioning Knowledge Rubric Generator: **http://pamhook.com/solo-apps/functioning-knowledge-rubric-generator**

Differentiating learning intentions to challenge all learners

You can use SOLO to design differentiated learning intentions in a scheme of work (or student inquiry) using the process of constructive alignment, which creates learning tasks at different levels of cognitive complexity. Clarifying learning intentions (goals) helps to improve student achievement outcomes (Grant and Dweck 2003). For example, in the following scheme of work exploring pedestrian safety in the local community, the shift from unistructural to multistructural shows a quantitative increase in complexity, while the shift to relational and then on to extended abstract shows a qualitative increase.

Identify a "pedestrian crossing" on a local road. (Unistructural task)

Describe the crossing including any potential hazards to pedestrians. (Multistructural task)

Describe the pedestrians who use the crossing. (Multistructural task)

Compare and contrast how different pedestrians use the crossing. (Relational task)

Classify the pedestrians on the basis of how they use the crossing. (Relational task)

Predict the pedestrian group who are most at risk when using the crossing. (Extended abstract task)

Explain why the pedestrian group seems most at risk. (Relational task)

Justify why the pedestrian group seems most at risk. (Extended abstract task)

Plan an action to help manage the perceived risk to the pedestrians using the crossing. (Extended abstract task)

Task: Design up to five learning intentions to help students increase the complexity of their understanding of "change" in a context of your own choosing. For example, it might involve change in a character, political system, geographical feature, technological outcome, living organism, setting or musical genre. For online help, go to the HookED Learning Intention Generator: http://pamhook.com/solo-apps/learning-intention-generator

Measuring complexity of learning task and outcome independently

With SOLO, teachers and students can describe the successful completion of a task at many levels of complexity. Regardless of its own complexity, any task can have outcomes at different SOLO levels.

If SOLO is used to differentiate success criteria for any learning intention (LI), all students can experience success when completing a task and to be challenged to imagine the next step. The following Tables 2.8–2.10 show how SOLO has been used to differentiate three of the learning intentions from the pedestrian crossing example introduced in the section above.

Table 2.8: SOLO self-assessment rubric for LI: Describe the pedestrians who use the crossing (multistructural task)

	Prestructural	Unistructural	Multistructural	Relational	Extended abstract
Pedestrian safety					
What are they like?	I need help to describe the pedestrians.	My description has one relevant characteristic or attribute.	My description has several relevant characteristics or attributes ...	... and I provide reasons for these characteristics or attributes ...	... and I make a generalisation based on the characteristics or attributes.

See Section 3 for examples of SOLO maps and self-assessment rubrics.

Table 2.9: SOLO self-assessment rubric for LI: Classify the pedestrians on the basis of how they use the crossing (relational task)

	Prestructural	Unistructural	Multistructural	Relational	Extended abstract
Pedestrian safety					
What groups or types are there?	I need help to classify the pedestrians.	My classification forms one relevant group.	My classification forms several relevant groups and subgroups …	… **and** I provide reasons for these groups and subgroups …	… **and** I make a generalisation based on the groups I have made.

Table 2.10: SOLO self-assessment rubric for LI: Justify why the pedestrian group seems most at risk (extended abstract task)

	Prestructural	Unistructural	Multistructural	Relational	Extended abstract
Pedestrian safety					
What reasons and evidence do you have?	I need help to justify a claim.	I can explain (give a reason) why it is reasonable to hold that a claim is true. *because*	I can elaborate on the meaning of my explanation as to why a claim is true … *by this I mean*	… **and** I can provide reasons for my reasons in support of my explanation … [reliability] *because*	… **and** I can provide evidence in support of my justification. [validity]

Task: Answer the question, "What is teaching as inquiry like?" (multistructural task designed to bring in ideas) with sample responses set at different levels of SOLO Taxonomy. Each response should add to the quantitative and/or qualitative complexity of the previous response.

Extended abstract response	
Relational response	
Multistructural response	
Unistructural response	
Prestructural response	

Setting explicit, proximate and hierarchical learning goals

Vygotsky (1978) refers to the distance between the student's current level of understanding (what is known) and their level of potential development (what is not known). His **zone of proximal development** is the zone where the skills needed are too difficult for a student to master on their own but within their reach with support, guidance and encouragement from teachers and/or peers. Setting explicit, proximate and hierarchical learning goals is key to this process.

Mediating a student's learning activity is often referred to as **scaffolding**. Silver (2011) suggests that, when scaffolding, the teacher:

- assesses the student's current knowledge and experience of the academic content
- relates the content to what the student already understands or can do
- breaks a task into small, more manageable tasks with opportunities for intermittent feedback
- uses verbal cues and prompts to assist the student.

If we apply SOLO levels to students' understanding, it is easier to determine their current knowledge and the elements of the learning task that are beyond their capability. We can use SOLO "+ 1" as a guide to introduce new elements that are within their range of competence – that is, one SOLO level further on from their current level of understanding. For example, if a test of prior knowledge shows a group of students has a multistructural understanding of the topic, you can set the task one level ahead, at a relational level. Table 2.11 offers an example from a novel study.

Table 2.11: Using the SOLO "+ 1" approach to set explicit, proximate and hierarchical learning goals

Novel	*Of Mice and Men* by John Steinbeck
Student task	**List causes** of the Great Depression. [Multistructural task]
Initial student outcome	A major cause of the Great Depression was the stock market crash in the United States on Black Tuesday, 29 October 1929. Bank closures and a general reduction in spending were contributing causes. [Multistructural outcome because student simply lists causes]
New learning goal using the + 1 prompt	
Student task	**Explain why** the stock market crash, bank closures and a general reduction in spending caused the Great Depression. [Relational task: + 1 prompt]
New student outcome	A major cause of the Great Depression was the stock market crash in the United States on Black Tuesday, 29 October 1929. This is a cause because the collapse led the stockholders to lose over $40 billion. When attempts to call in loans failed, bank closures followed and, because bank deposits were uninsured when the banks failed, many people lost all their savings. The stock market crash created uncertainty and pessimism. Because they were fearful of further economic problems, people from all walks of life lost confidence and reduced their spending on everyday items. This loss in demand led to a reduction in crop prices, a loss in production, a loss in tax revenue and an increase in bankruptcies and unemployment. It was an extended period of widespread poverty, hunger, homelessness and despair. A period of severe drought in the 1930s (the Dust Bowl) added to this despair, forcing tens of thousands of families to abandon their farms. [Relational outcome because student identifies and explains causes]

We can also use the "+ 1" approach when designing differentiated tasks for SOLO station activities (see Figure 2.4). As with other SOLO strategies, students can be shown how to think about their own next steps using the + 1 approach and design their own next steps.

Task: Working with a colleague, exchange a sample of student work. Use SOLO to determine the level of cognitive complexity shown by the outcomes. Use the + 1 strategy to design a task that will be explicit, proximate and hierarchical for the students involved in producing the work samples. Share your decisions and actions with the colleague. Do they agree or disagree with your decisions? Do you agree or disagree with theirs? Discuss your decisions and seek consensus.

A useful, quick measure of prior knowledge for students and teachers

Both teachers and students can identify a student's existing level of understanding using:

- open-ended tasks
- SOLO-differentiated questions, prompts or tasks
- SOLO hexagons.

You can also get an approximate gauge of students' self-assessed SOLO level by asking the class to communicate through hand signs, as in Figure 2.2.

Task: Ask your students to draw an annotated diagram showing what they already know about a topic you are about to teach. Encourage them to look at the drawings of other students and add something to their drawing. Students can work in pairs to self-assess the levels of their prior knowledge. Ask them to justify their assessment and make a suggestion about their next step. Check the drawings to see if you agree or disagree with the students' assessments. Share your thinking with the students.

Source: Lincoln High School, Canterbury, New Zealand

A nuanced language for metacognitive reflection

When we share SOLO with students, we give them a model and a vocabulary that opens up nuanced conversation about learning and learning outcomes. It gives them a language of "stuckedness" that they can use to more clearly discuss what is holding them back in their learning. Students and their teachers sharing this powerfully explicit model of learning have a common language to talk about their learning outcomes at surface, deep and conceptual levels. Indeed, Hattie (2012) describes SOLO as "the most powerful model for understanding these levels and integrating them into learning intentions and success criteria" (p 54).

Students and teachers can therefore use the language of SOLO to reflect on what students are doing, how well it is going and what the next steps are. For example, if you use SOLO to make learning intentions and success criteria visible with students, your students can then use SOLO levels to support nuanced reflection. Table 2.12 offers an example.

Table 2.12: Using the language of SOLO for metacognitive reflection

Reflective question	Student response
What am I doing?	I am watching a DVD video of *The Hollow Crown: Richard II* to help me describe the landscapes and architecture of the period. This is a multistructural task because I am collecting loose ideas about the attributes and characteristics of the period.
How well is it going?	It is going well. I have several new ideas about the architecture of the period and have made links between these and the current day. This is a relational outcome because I have been able to relate the landscape and architecture of the past and present, finding similarities and differences.
What should I do next?	I am going to read some different resources to find out more about medieval timber architecture and determine the extent of the influence of the past on modern design. My first step will be to read more widely to bring in more relevant ideas – a multistructural task. When I determine the influence of the past, I will be looking for causal effects, a relational task, but when I am determining the importance of these effects on modern design the task will be evaluative at an extended abstract level.

Task: Reflect on your professional practice. Choose an area of your pedagogical content knowledge you would like to focus on with others. Identify a series of professional readings that will support the group's learning. Think about your thinking using SOLO levels when discussing the articles with other members of your professional learning group. Share your reflections with your colleagues. Help students think about their thinking in similar ways using the "what am I doing; how well is it going; what should I do next" prompts and SOLO levels.

A framework for assessing a student's declarative knowledge

After learning to code assessment questions at different levels of SOLO, students highlight and annotate their notes with questions that could be asked about the topic. In this revision strategy, students ask questions at multistructural, relational and extended abstract levels.

For example, after reading a section of text, students ask themselves:

- What are the questions that I might be asked to test my understanding of loose ideas?
- What are the questions that I might be asked to test my ability to relate or link ideas?
- What are the questions that I might be asked to test my ability to think about the wider implications of the topic?

Figure 2.3 presents an approach that one student has taken.

Figure 2.3: Student-generated revision questions at different levels of SOLO

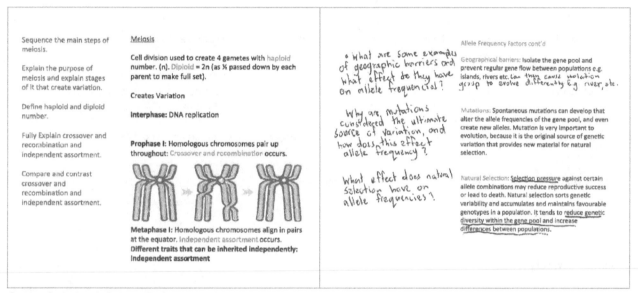

Source: St Andrew's College, Christchurch, New Zealand

Task: Challenge students to contribute their own questions (and answers) to a shared class revision sheet. The worksheet questions should be designed to test understanding at different levels of SOLO.

A clear indication of student progress in learning across a lesson or topic

With activities that incorporate SOLO levels, teachers and students can clearly identify what understanding students have gained over a given period of time. The following examples illustrate how it is possible to track progress with:

- SOLO station activities, which include SOLO hexagons and SOLO self-assessment rubrics (Figure 2.4)
- two options for entry and exit cards (Figures 2.5 and 2.6)
- HookED SOLO 5 (Figure 2.7), which uses a SOLO-differentiated series of questions to prompt students to reflect in increasingly deeper ways. This tool is often used as an exit card strategy.

Unistructural station

Tasks

- **Name** the event.
- **Draw** an annotated sketch of the event.
- **Identify** when the event occurred.
- **Identify** where the event occurred.
- **Identify** who was directly involved in the event.
- **Identify** who was indirectly involved in the event.
- **SOLO hexagons:** Curate the detail above on to separate SOLO hexagons.

SOLO self-assessment rubric for unistructural station activities

Extended abstract		... **and** I can work with others to help them identify the event and all the important detail.
Relational		I can identify the event (when and where it occurred and who was involved) ...
Multistructural		I can identify the event (when and where it occurred and who was involved) but I am not sure if I have got all the relevant detail correct.
Unistructural		I can identify the event (when and where it occurred and who was involved) if I am directed.
Prestructural		I need help to identify the event (when and where it occurred and who was involved).

Multistructural station

Tasks

- **List** three characters who hold views about this event.
- **Describe** the view of the event held by one of the three characters.
- **Describe** one action this character has taken in relation to the event.
  [Repeat this process for the other two characters.]
- **SOLO hexagons:** Add this detail on separate SOLO hexagons as done previously.

SOLO self-assessment rubric for multistructural station activities

Extended abstract		... **and** I make a generalisation about the character's views and/or actions.
Relational		... **and** I explain why these ideas are relevant ...
Multistructural		My description has several relevant ideas ...
Unistructural		My description has one relevant idea.
Prestructural		I need help to describe the character's view and/or action.

continued ...

30

Relational station

Tasks

- **Explain** why each character chose to take a particular action.
- **SOLO hexagons:** Add each character's reasons to separate hexagons. Create a tessellation by looking for connections between individual hexagons and annotate any links with reasons. Take a digital photo or video of your tessellation and include the reasons for relating ideas.

SOLO self-assessment rubric for relational station activities

Extended abstract	... **and** I can make a generalisation about the reasons why the character acted in certain ways.
Relational	... **and** I can justify these reasons ...
Multistructural	I can give several reasons why a character chose to take action ...
Unistructural	I can give a reason why a character chose to take action.
Prestructural	I need help to explain why a character chose to take action.

Extended abstract station

Tasks

- **Discuss** how the three characters' views and actions might change if this event was to take place in another place or at a different time.
- **SOLO hexagons:** Step back from the tessellation and make a generalisation about the event and the different perspectives held: "Overall I think ... because ... because ..."

SOLO self-assessment rubric for extended abstract station activities

Extended abstract	... **and** I can provide evidence to validate my claim.
Relational	... **and** I can justify my claim with reasons ...
Multistructural	I can make a generalisation and elaborate on it to clarify meaning ...
Unistructural	I can make a generalisation.
Prestructural	I need help to make a generalisation about the event and the different perspectives held.

Figure 2.5: Entry and exit cards for student reflection

Student name:	**Topic:**
Entry	**Exit**
Insert photo of HOT SOLO Define map or SOLO hexagons activity from prior knowledge task at the start of the topic.	Insert photo of HOT SOLO Define map or SOLO hexagons activity at the end of the topic.
My learning outcome is at ______________________	My learning outcome is at ______________________
because ______________________ ______________________ ______________________	because ______________________ ______________________ ______________________
My next step is to ______________________ ______________________ ______________________	My next step is to ______________________ ______________________ ______________________
My reflection on how and why my learning has changed:	

My progress: Entry and exit				
Name:	**Topic:**	**Date:**	**My SOLO level**	
Entry				
Prior knowledge: **What I know already:**	**Peer knowledge: What someone else knows:**			
	Next steps: What I need to know more about:			
Exit				
What I now know:	**What I need to know more about:**			
	Next steps: What I need to do next:			

Source: Template adapted from Smith and Turner (undated)

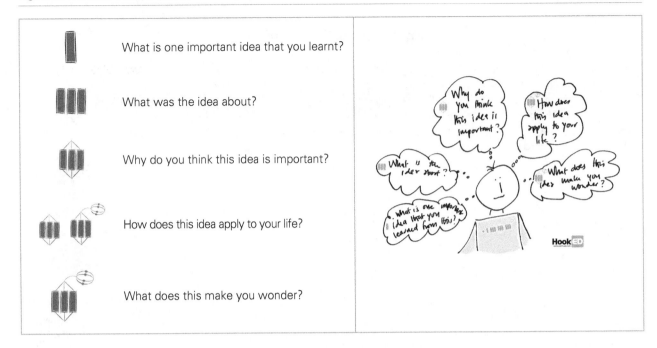

Task: Interview a group of students about how they know if they are making progress in their learning. Ask them for specific examples from their class work. Ask a group of teachers how, when they are teaching, they determine the extent to which students are progressing. Look for commonalities between the approaches of teachers and students.

A framework for thinking about questions, questioning and questioners

We can use SOLO to formulate questions that prompt responses at different levels of cognitive complexity. These questions may be:

- **multistructural** questions designed to bring in ideas – What is it? What is it like? What is it about?
- **relational** questions designed to prompt the linking of ideas – What caused it? What is a consequence? How is it similar or different? In what order does it happen? What is it similar to?
- **extended abstract** questions designed to extend students' relational thinking – How effective was this? What does this make you wonder? What will this look like in the future? What was the overall message?

For example, we can use question prompts for different levels of SOLO in oral discussion with students and when designing SOLO-differentiated worksheets, SOLO station activities and SOLO exit cards (as illustrated in the section above).

Similarly we can use SOLO to categorise the level of complexity of questions from both students and teachers. The following examples set out templates designed to capture:

- a teacher's questions during one or more lessons, coded against SOLO levels, to give the teacher feedback on the balance of surface and deep knowledge questions they asked (Table 2.13)
- a teacher's reflection on the types of questions students ask, coded against SOLO levels (Table 2.14).

These templates can be readily adapted for students to use in order to gauge the balance of surface and deep knowledge questions they ask and to reflect on the types of questions teachers ask, coded against SOLO levels.

Task: Ask a colleague to sit in on your class and record the questions you ask students and the questions students ask you across the lesson. Reflect on the ratio of different questions asked across the lesson and how appropriate this is for the content and context.

Table 2.13: Teacher observation and reflection – thinking about my questions

What type of questions do I ask during a lesson?

Log your questions and code them against SOLO levels.

| Questions asked over a lesson | Code SOLO level of each question | | |
	Unistructural or multistructural Bringing in ideas	Relational Linking ideas	Extended abstract
Total questions asked			
Teacher reflection on how well the type of questions asked meets the learning needs of students			

Table 2.14: Teacher observation and reflection – thinking about my students' questions

What type of questions do my students ask during a lesson?

Log the questions your students ask during a lesson and code them against SOLO levels.

| Questions asked over a lesson | Code SOLO level of each question | | |
	Unistructural or multistructural Bringing in ideas	Relational Linking ideas	Extended abstract
Total questions asked			
Teacher reflection on the type of questions their students ask during a lesson			

3. How can we apply SOLO in the classroom?

We are supposed to wait until senior management meets and decides on how this will happen. But I'm not that patient. I can see how sharing SOLO will help my students develop a "growth mindset" – and I am starting first thing tomorrow morning.
Teacher after a SOLO Taxonomy Teacher Only Day

SOLO is a model that focuses on the learning outcome. Given that everything we do in schools is focused on the learner and the learning outcome, SOLO is useful in everything we do. The choice means some teachers immediately see how SOLO will address a need for their students and jump right in. Others feel overwhelmed by choice when deciding how, where and when to start using the model with students in their classrooms.

The introduction of SOLO as a model of learning should always follow the discussion on why you want to introduce it. Without identifying a clear purpose (or a need that SOLO might help address), we risk cluttering the complex job of teaching and learning with yet another "good idea" that detracts from effective practice.

Identifying a need that a common model of learning might answer (or a reason from those listed in Section 2) is a good place to start. Knowing what you intend to change is the first step in designing research (quantitative or qualitative) to measure whether you achieve that change. And this requires capturing a snapshot or baseline of the student's learning you hope to change before you start.

> **Tip: Start simply and start small**
>
> Whatever the narrative, my advice is to start simply and on a small scale. For example, you could start by using SOLO terms, symbols and hand signs to indicate and explain the level of complexity of tasks and outcomes across a lesson.
>
> Making learning visible in this way does not require any special budget, photocopying, laminated wall displays, handouts or Post-it notes. Starting with learning intentions and success criteria involves labelling what you already do so that students can see the structure of the task and outcome. You can make symbols online with the HookED SOLO Symbol Generator (http://pamhook.com/solo-apps/solo-symbol-generator).

Introducing SOLO as a model for learning in the classroom

Here are some of the many, many ways to introduce SOLO as a model of learning.

Mindset

SOLO emphasises effort, strategies and making mistakes when learning. I often talk to teachers and students about SOLO in the context of Carol Dweck's "growth mindset" (Dweck 1999, 2006) and "one line of praise studies" (Cimpian et al 2007; Kamins and Dweck 1999; Mueller and Dweck 1998). In emphasising the importance of seeing effort as a positive aspect of learning (Blackwell et al 2007; Nussbaum and Dweck 2008), I stress that a learner needs a clear understanding of what they are doing, how well it is going and what their next steps for learning are and how they can achieve this through using SOLO.

Learning to do something

You can introduce SOLO by making an analogy between the model and the process of learning how to skateboard, play a team sport, perform a piece of music, feed yourself yoghurt or construct a dwelling on Minecraft (Figure 3.1).

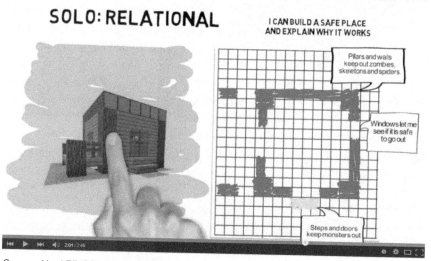

Source: HookED SOLO Taxonomy Minecraft (http://youtu.be/4XrxiHHHaQA)

Rodney Mullen's skateboard videos (search using his name on YouTube) provide great examples of what an extended abstract performance might entail. Being able to transfer the skills of feeding yourself yoghurt to another setting is an example of an extended abstract outcome for a student in a special needs environment. It is obvious in every case that this extended abstract outcome has come from effort and hours and hours of practice with the use of different effective strategies – not luck or fixed ability.

SOLO hexagons

Using SOLO hexagons is a great hands-on way to demonstrate that loose ideas are important but become more interesting when you can make connections between them and more powerful again when you can step back and see the "big picture" (Figure 3.2). If you are using this activity to introduce SOLO as a model, it is best to use a topic that teachers, students and/or families are already very familiar with – for example, the holidays, morning tea or a recent community issue.

For more information, see "Introducing SOLO through systems thinking and SOLO hexagons" (p 36).

Figure 3.2: SOLO hexagons as a hands-on way to demonstrate the power of making connections and seeing the big picture

Source: Wellesley College, Wellington, New Zealand

Labelling learning intentions

By labelling learning intentions, you create a great context for teaching students the symbols and hand signs for each level and for encouraging students to use them in learning conversations across each day. You might have separate SOLO symbols (laminated) with a movable arrow on the whiteboard to code learning intentions, questions, student responses and so on (Figure 3.3). Alternatively you might use SOLO hand signs to familiarise students with the different levels, as in the following example:

> We have just watched a DVD about the effects of ecotourism on the Galapagos Islands. What is your level of understanding about the outcomes we saw in the documentary? If you think you can list several effects of ecotourism, use the multistructural hand sign for loose ideas, like this [shows sign]. If you can explain why these are direct or indirect consequences of ecotourism using connectives like "because", then use the relational hand sign for connected ideas – like this [show sign].

Figure 3.3: Labelling SOLO learning intentions on the whiteboard

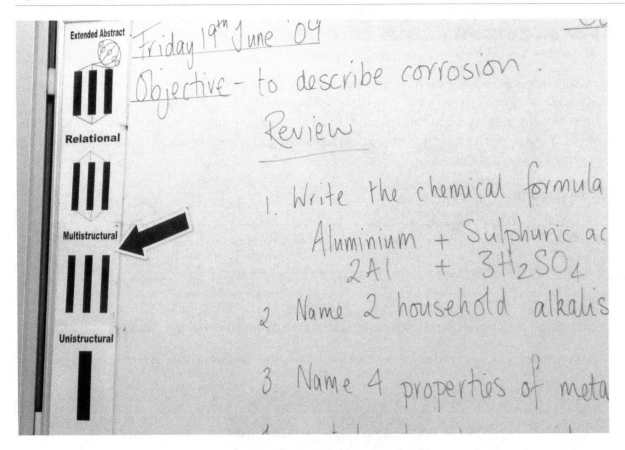

Labelling success criteria and identifying next steps

As noted in previous sections, the cognitive complexity of the task and outcome can be at different SOLO levels. For example, a multistructural task (eg, *describe*) can be achieved at unistructural, multistructural, relational and extended abstract levels.

When thinking about the intended learning outcomes at the start of an activity, it is useful to indicate the SOLO level of the success criteria. To do so, you need to use SOLO levels consistently to describe the cognitive complexity of learning tasks (learning intentions), outcomes (success criteria) and next steps – and to encourage students to contribute. For example:

> Today we are starting to explore and then describe the social norms that exist when people upload photos to a social networking site. Who would like to suggest a suitable learning intention? What is the SOLO level of the task? Why do you think that? How will we know we are successful? What levels of success are there?

Aligning academic verbs with SOLO levels in learning intentions (LI) and success criteria (SC) helps to create a common language for learning.

LI: [verb] [content] [context] – SOLO level of task

SC: Outlined at different levels of SOLO

SOLO stickers and stamps

You can use SOLO stickers and stamps to help students learn to self-assess the level of their learning outcome, justify their choice and suggest next steps. Figure 3.4 offers a template for self-assessment with HookED SOLO stickers or stamps; Figure 3.5 shows how some students have completed the assessment with their reflections and their choice of sticker that reflects the SOLO level of their learning outcome.

Figure 3.4: Template for self-assessment with HookED SOLO stickers or stamps

My learning outcome is at	My learning outcome is at
because _____	because _____
My next step is to _____	My next step is to _____

Figure 3.5: Examples of how students have used SOLO stickers or stamps

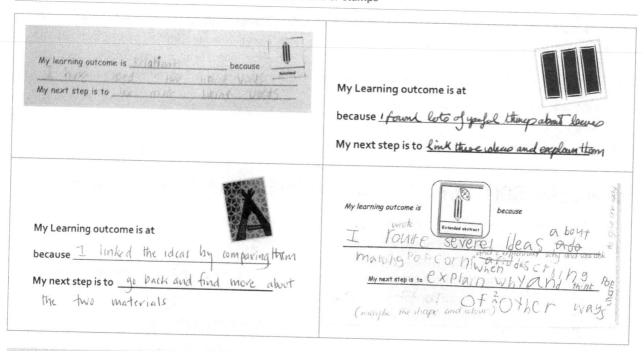

Wall displays

To reinforce your signing and talking about the SOLO level of a learning task and success criteria, you can use wall displays. Many schools purchase and/or create posters, banners and flipcharts with SOLO symbols, hand signs and verbs for display and reference in every learning area (Figure 3.6).

Figure 3.6: Poster of HookED SOLO hand signs and learning verbs

Sharing the load

The next step is to involve students, making the class collectively responsible for:

- classifying the SOLO level of the tasks they undertake across a day

- differentiating the success criteria for those tasks.

By being actively involved, students will develop fluency and flexibility when thinking about learning outcomes that show the SOLO structures of one relevant idea, several relevant ideas, connected ideas or extended ideas. To do this, it is useful to first distinguish between functioning and declarative knowledge (see Section 1).

From here it is a small step to work with students to co-construct SOLO-differentiated success criteria for tasks. What would your learning outcome for this task look like at the unistructural, multistructural, relational or extended abstract level? The activity of sharing the construction process with students helps to build their understanding and fluency in using SOLO levels to self-assess their own learning and suggest next steps. Some schools engage students in:

- creating freeze-frame drama images of student learning outcomes to capture the differentiated success criteria for learning tasks

- creating SOLO comic strip rubrics for the tasks that matter most.

Introducing SOLO through systems thinking and SOLO hexagons

Using SOLO hexagons[1] provides insight into the cognitive understanding different students have before, during and after activities for learning (prior knowledge, formative and summative assessment for learning). You can then use this insight when you are designing further learning activities to both support and challenge students. The hexagon activity itself can prompt students to think more deeply about concepts and big ideas and to undertake systems thinking about complex issues. It is also widely used as a revision strategy.

In this strategy for generating and connecting ideas, the students work individually or in collaborative groups.

Teachers and/or students can prepare the content on the hexagons before the session or generate it during the session. You may use:

- a wide range of content, such as text, quotes, symbols, images, photographs, graphs, tables, equations, geometric shapes and political cartoons

- different-coloured hexagons to represent different categories of content.

---

1   SOLO hexagons are based on an idea from Hodgson (1992).

Process for student-generated content

Where students are generating the hexagon content, ask them to:

- **brainstorm** everything they know about a given topic (presented as a focus question)
- **record** each idea or thought on a separate blank hexagon by writing text or drawing images
- **make links between** the hexagons by tessellating them
- **annotate with the reasons** for linking the hexagons
- **make a generalisation** about the tessellation.

As Figure 3.7 indicates, you can curate the tessellation in a digital photo, which you can then use as a scaffold for oral discussion or a future written text.

To extend student thinking, once they have completed the initial activity, introduce extra hexagons with prompts for students to think in new ways.

Figure 3.7: A digital record of a SOLO hexagon tessellation can scaffold further learning

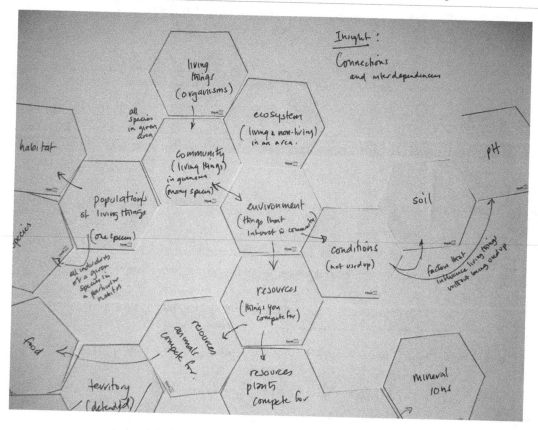

Outcomes of SOLO hexagon activity

The outcome differs according to the SOLO level (Figure 3.8):

- In a **multistructural** outcome, students can describe the content on the individual hexagons.
- In a **relational** outcome, students can make straight-edge connections between simple hexagon sequences and clusters. They can tessellate the hexagons (making connections) and explain why they have linked the ideas together in this way (talk or annotate).
- In an **extended abstract** outcome, students can explore the node where three hexagons share a corner (or simply look at a cluster of hexagons). They can step away from all the linked ideas and make a generalisation about the nature of the relationship between the ideas. This step involves extending what is known in a new way.

Figure 3.8: HookED SOLO hexagons rubric

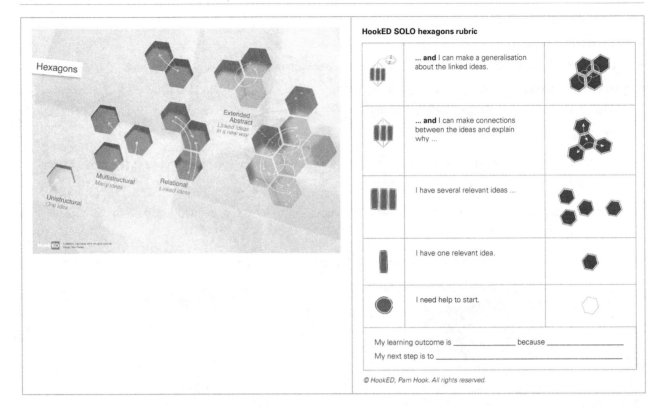

Reasons for starting to use SOLO hexagons

You may start using hexagons for any of the following reasons:

1. **Introduce SOLO as a model.** SOLO hexagons are a great way to introduce students of all ages to SOLO as a model of learning outcomes.

2. **Determine prior knowledge.** You can use SOLO hexagons to determine a student's depth of prior knowledge and understanding before starting to learn. The approach is similar to a brainstorming activity except with SOLO hexagons you spend time looking for connections between the ideas and then step back and make a generalisation or "big picture" claim. The content of the hexagons may be student-generated, identified by the teacher as relevant to the topic, or a mix of both. Where students are generating the content, ask them to:
   - draw or write everything they know about the topic on to separate hexagons (an indicator of multistructural understanding)
   - work in pairs or small groups to find links or connections between the loose ideas (an indicator of relational understanding)
   - step back from the various tessellations and make a "big picture" call about the essence or significance of the topic (an indicator of extended abstract understanding).

   You can test this understanding further by offering students hexagons you have prepared with prompts to consider the political, social, economic, environmental or cultural implications of the topic. Alternatively you could give them prepared hexagons and ask them to describe each one and to make and annotate connections between them as above.

3. **Scaffold student writing.** Students can use their annotated tessellations as prompts for their writing. Sometimes the students write from the tessellation itself; more commonly they write from a digital photo of the tessellation (as in Figure 3.7 on the previous page).

4. **Conduct formative assessment.** Students can add to, revise and reorganise tessellations they created at the beginning of a topic. Using different-coloured hexagons and annotations helps differentiate new thinking.

5. **Revise and/or extend student thinking.** Prepare hexagons before the lesson to extend your students' thinking beyond the initial connections made. Effective strategies are to: print hexagons on different-coloured paper; ask students to add quotes or elaborations on the back of hexagons (turning them into flip cards); or ask them to guess the content on a flipped or blank hexagon.

> **Tip: So much and no more**
>
> When learning to use SOLO hexagons for systems thinking with students, do not assume it will automatically lead to extended abstract learning outcomes. Students who start with very little relevant content knowledge will struggle to make relevant connections etc. Just as it is possible to "over-SOLO-map" and "over-rubric" students, it is possible to over-use SOLO hexagons. It is only one of many pedagogical approaches available to classroom teachers.

SOLO hexagon resources

Resources available for your SOLO hexagon activities are:

- the online HookED SOLO Hexagon Generator (**http://pamhook.com/solo-apps/hexagon-generator**), which you can use to add content to hexagons. Once this tool has generated the Word document, it is possible to add images, photographs, colour, different fonts etc
- SOLO hexagon templates (**http://pamhook.com/wiki/SOLO_Hexagons**), including a larger template for younger students
- SOLO hexagon template and examples from early years settings (Hook and Cassé 2013, pp 13–14)
- SOLO hexagon concept mapping (McNeill and Hook 2012, p 7)
- SOLO reverse hexagons (Hook et al 2014, p 40).

> **Tip: Develop your ideas about SOLO hexagons with colleagues**
>
> When starting out with SOLO hexagons, bring samples of your students' learning outcomes to a staff meeting and share the strengths and weaknesses of this pedagogical approach with colleagues. Teachers in New Zealand and the United Kingdom have found many ways to further develop the strategy in this way.

Introducing SOLO as part of the academic language of the classroom

Language matters. There is little point in telling students that relating their ideas, explaining causes and making comparisons are all ways to show a deeper learning outcome if they do not know how to relate ideas, explain or compare. Many students need help to clarify what to do when responding to different task descriptors.

Clarifying the SOLO level of the academic verb used in a task is an important first step in identifying the intent of the verb. To do this, we must ask which academic verbs we commonly use in our school when we want students to:

- bring in ideas (multistructural task)
- relate ideas (relational task)
- extend ideas (extended abstract task).

This section shows how SOLO visual process maps and supporting self-assessment rubrics are a start-up language resource that can support students' thinking processes as they respond to a given academic verb. It includes a selection of templates of HOT and HookED SOLO maps and rubrics, along with instructions on how to use them.

See Hook and Mills (2011) for other HOT SOLO maps. Visual self-assessment rubrics, based on the HOT SOLO and HookED SOLO maps, are also available (Hook and Mills 2011). They lighten the text load for students who are self-assessing their outcomes.

How visual process maps can help

Students need to know the overall purpose of each verb, which may require them to:

- bring in ideas, such as *define* and *describe*

- relate ideas, such as *classify* and *explain causes*

- extend ideas, such as *generalise* and *evaluate*.

More than that, however, they need support in learning how to structure their thinking in response to it. For example, explaining causes and classifying are both ways of linking ideas but one involves finding reasons or causes while the other involves looking for commonalities and grouping.

The SOLO visual process maps help to anchor students' ideas and thinking in ways that mimic the steps involved in the process of acting on each verb. In this way, they reduce the cognitive load of understanding the task and, with practice, allow complex routines to become automatic.

It is well established that concept mapping supports effective learning (Buckner 2004; Novak 2013). As cognitive capacity is limited, the maps promote learning by freeing students from puzzling over the nature of the task and the ideas they bring to the task so that they can instead focus on the ideas and the relationship between them. They allow an automaticity equivalent to having fluency (or automatic recall) with basic maths facts, which allows students to use that information in other settings. As a nine-year-old student remarked:

> If it is possible to fall in love with a map then I am in love with the Describe map and the way it helps me remember my ideas when I am writing.

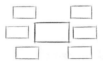

The maps prompt for surface, deep and conceptual understanding. They also help students structure their writing in simple sentences, complex sentences and paragraphs.

Combining HOT and HookED SOLO maps with self-assessment rubrics

Each SOLO map comes with a self-assessment rubric that you share with students when they write from the map. By listing success criteria at each SOLO level, the rubrics encourage students to structure their answers in ways that represent deeper thinking (see Section 2). The simplicity of the SOLO levels means students can co-construct these rubrics with teachers and, after some practice, make their own.

Schools make SOLO maps and rubrics available in different ways, such as by:

- providing class sets of SOLO maps and rubrics

- including them in every student's homework diary

- presenting them in wall displays.

As a classroom resource, the SOLO maps and rubrics provide a common toolbox of strategies to help students think at different levels of SOLO. Figure 3.9 shows a student referring to a SOLO self-assessment rubric when writing. Figures 3.10 and 3.11 illustrate some of the range of maps and rubrics that are available.

Once students are fluent in using the SOLO maps and rubrics, they can analyse exemplars of students' responses to the maps. By highlighting the sections of the text that show loose ideas, connected ideas or extended ideas and the connectives involved at each level, students develop a clearer understanding of what it is about the structure of a piece of text that gives it a relational or extended abstract outcome. From this, they learn to take text at one SOLO level and modify it so that it shows the structure of the level above or the level below.

Figure 3.9: Using the HookED SOLO Describe ++ rubric to self-assess work

Source: Edendale Primary School, Auckland, New Zealand

Figure 3.10: A set of HOT SOLO maps

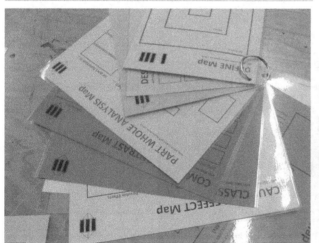

Figure 3.11: A set of HOT SOLO self-assessment rubrics

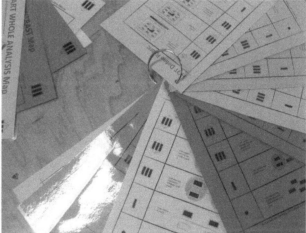

Tip: More information on SOLO maps and self-assessment rubrics

HookED "How to ..." SOLO map YouTube videos: www.youtube.com/user/Chokearti

HookED postcard-sized versions of the maps and self-assessment rubrics, available from HookED:
http://pamhook.com/contact

HookED Issuu slideshows (http://pamhook.com/presentations) on:

- HOT SOLO maps and SOLO Taxonomy
- SOLO Taxonomy and assessing student thinking
- SOLO Taxonomy, HOT SOLO maps and metacognition.

HookED SOLO Describe ++ resources

A SOLO multi-level map, the HookED SOLO Describe ++ map (Figure 3.12), is sometimes called "the one map to rule them all". Figure 3.13 presents the accompanying self-assessment rubric.

Describe ++ What can you see? Why do you think it is like that? What does it make you wonder?

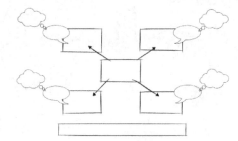

What are these resources for? You can use the HookED Describe ++ map and self-assessment rubric to help students describe, explain and generalise. The map scaffolds students' thinking at multistructural, relational and extended abstract levels and supports both surface and deep features when students write from the map through:

- scaffolding for sentence structure (simple and complex) and paragraphing
- increasing the number of ideas presented
- deepening the quality of ideas presented.

The map improves students' observational powers in many different contexts, such as when viewing artworks, political cartoons, digital images, moving images, static images, graphs, line equations, tables, maths and science problems and science experiments. The loose ideas are related to other ideas in the speech bubble with prompts of "Why do you think it is like that?" and the connectives "because" and "so that". This step prompts science students to make inferences about their observations and prompts students in other contexts to suggest causal explanations. The final extended abstract prompt is represented by the thought bubble and by prompts such as, "What does this make you wonder? How effective is this? Overall how did this make you feel?"

How do I use these resources? Follow this step-by-step guide in which you lead students through the process of responding to the map before they try it for themselves, guided by the success criteria in the self-assessment rubric.

1. Align the HookED SOLO Describe ++ map and self-assessment rubric with the identified learning intention. For example, "We are learning to describe in depth [content] [context]."
2. Place the idea or object to be described in the centre of the map.
3. Suggest possible attributes for the description.
4. Record the relevant attributes in the "characteristic" rectangles that sit around the main idea (multistructural listing).
5. In the speech bubbles attached to each rectangle, explain the identified characteristics. Why do you think it is like that? For example, "This is like this because …" and "This is like this so that …" (relational explanation).
6. Make a generalisation about each attribute. What does it make you wonder? How effective is this? How does this make you feel? For example, "Overall this makes me wonder … because … because …"
7. Make a generalisation about the object and all the attributes. For example, "Overall I think … because … because …"
8. Share with the students the success criteria for the HookED SOLO Describe ++ rubric.
9. With reference to the success criteria, students create their own in-depth description of the idea using relevant characteristics and the target vocabulary from the completed Describe ++ map. They may write or say these statements or convey them through an annotated drawing. This process is iterative, meaning that students can repeat it whenever new learning occurs and thus can improve on the original description.
10. Students self- or peer-assess their descriptions and seek teacher feedback on them.
11. Students assess their learning outcome for the identified learning intention against the SOLO levels, explain why they have chosen this level of learning outcome for their work (feedback) and suggest "where to next" steps (feed up).
12. Students record their work in a student learning log.

Figure 3.12: Template for HookED SOLO Describe ++ map

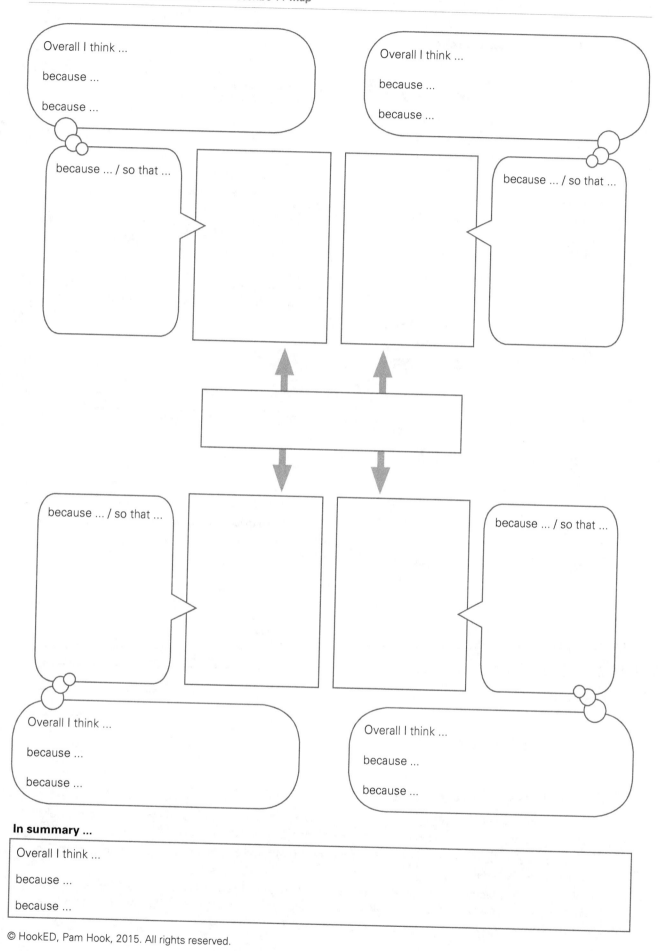

In summary ...

Overall I think ...

because ...

because ...

SOLO level	Learning outcome	
Extended abstract		My description identifies several relevant features, links these and makes a generalisation. It integrates these generalisations into a new understanding.
Relational		My description identifies several relevant features and links these by explanation.
Multistructural		My description identifies several relevant features.
Unistructural		My description identifies one relevant feature.
Prestructural		I need help to identify any relevant features.

My learning outcome is _____ because _____

_____

My next step is to _____

_____

Tip: It can help to break down the Describe ++ map

The HookED SOLO Describe ++ map provides a coherent overview of an idea. For students to use it effectively, it is sometimes necessary to break the map into smaller sections. You can do so by either:

- focusing on the attributes in the centre of the map (rectangles) and exposing the prompts for deeper thinking to students at a later date, or

- following a single attribute from rectangle to speech bubble to thought bubble, using a HookED SOLO thinking strip (Figure 3.14). This is a common approach in junior school classrooms (Figure 3.15). The prompts in the extended abstract level can be modified to suit your intended outcome.

Figure 3.14: Template for HookED SOLO thinking strips

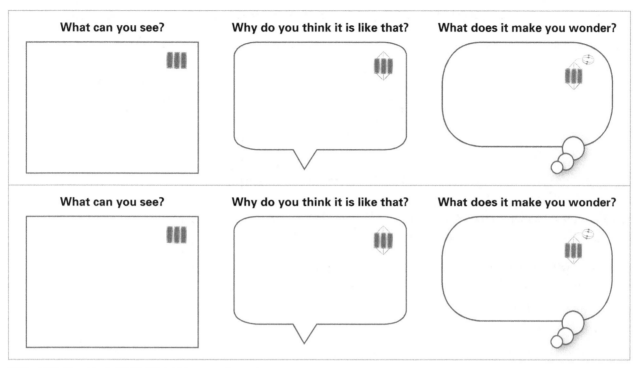

Figure 3.15: Example of a HookED SOLO writing strip in use in a primary school classroom

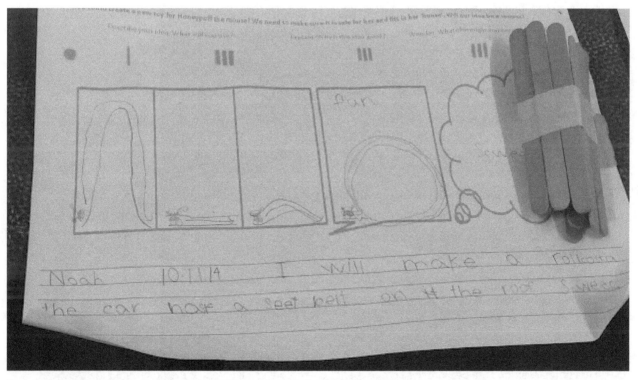

Source: Bridget Cassé's classroom at Edendale Primary School, Auckland, New Zealand

Process maps to bring in ideas (unistructural and multistructural maps)

Here we focus on the HOT SOLO Define map (Figure 3.16) and accompanying self-assessment rubric (Figure 3.17).

Other resources for bringing in ideas are the HOT SOLO Describe map and self-assessment rubric (Hook and Mills 2011).

Define – What is it?

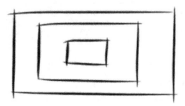

What are these resources for? You can use the HOT SOLO Define map and self-assessment rubric to clarify the meaning of unknown ideas, vocabulary and terms.

How do I use these resources? Follow this step-by-step guide in which you lead students through the process of responding to the map before they try it for themselves, guided by the success criteria in the self-assessment rubric.

1. Align the HOT SOLO Define map and self-assessment rubric with the identified learning intention. For example, "We are learning to define [content] [context]."

2. Place the idea to be defined (main idea) in the centre of the map.

3. Add ideas related to the main idea in the "relevant" middle rectangle.

4. Clarify these ideas with students and move ideas that are not relevant to the "not relevant" outer rectangle. Note: If the students have not generated many ideas, give them the opportunity to improve their content understanding through books, ICTs, guest speakers etc. Then add their new ideas to the map and discuss their relevance with students.

5. Explain the identified ideas and make links between them.

6. Make a generalisation about the idea. For example, "Overall ... because ... because ..."

7. Share with students the success criteria for definition in the HOT SOLO Define rubric.

8. With reference to the success criteria, students make their own definition statements using the ideas and the target vocabulary from the completed HOT SOLO Define map. They may draw, write or say these statements. This process is iterative, meaning that students can repeat it whenever new learning occurs and thus can improve on the original definition statement.

9. Students self- or peer-assess their definition statements and seek teacher feedback on them.

10. Students assess their learning outcome for the identified learning intention against the SOLO levels, explain why they have chosen this level of learning outcome for their work (feedback) and suggest "where to next" steps (feed up).

11. Students record this work in their learning logs.

Tip: Define every day

You can use the HOT SOLO Define map on a daily basis to develop new understandings of the topic you are teaching. After following the process above for one idea, place another idea in the centre box and move the words that are not relevant to that idea into the "not relevant" outer rectangle and repeat the process. In this way, as you add to the HOT SOLO Define map regularly, you start to build a contextual overview of the topic. By moving ideas and vocabulary in and out of the relevant box according to their relevance to the main idea, students also understand that defining involves sorting for relevance.

Not relevant

Relevant

Overall …

because …

because …

Figure 3.17: Template for HOT SOLO Define self-assessment rubric

SOLO level	Learning outcome	
Extended abstract 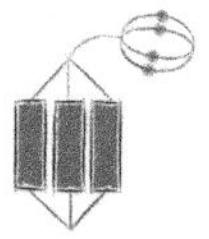	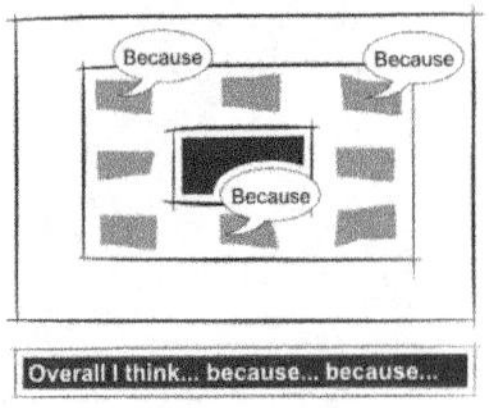	**... and** my definition looks at these ideas in a new way.
Relational 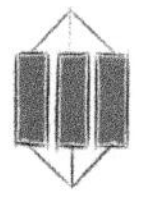	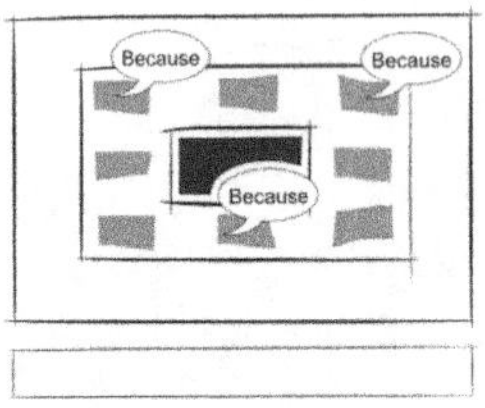	**... and** my definition links these ideas ...
Multistructural 	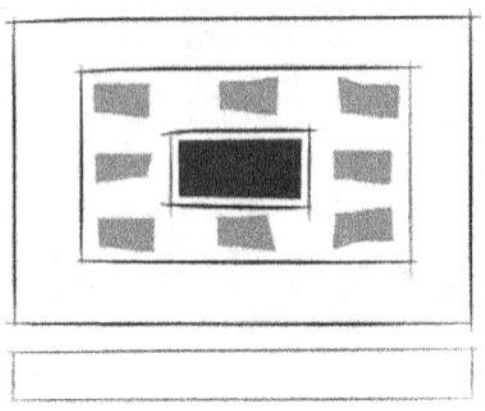	My definition has several relevant ideas about X ...
Unistructural 	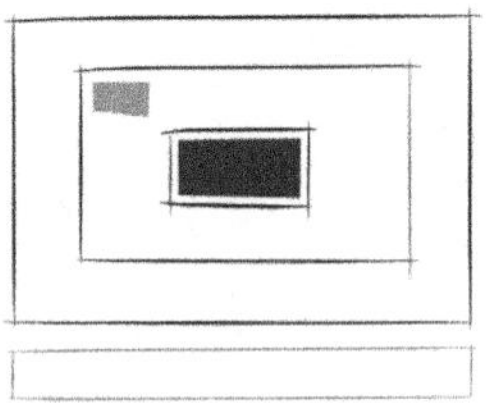	My definition has one relevant idea about X.
Prestructural 	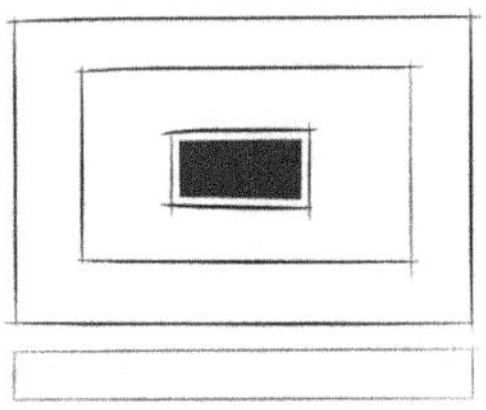	I need help to define X.

My definition statement is at a _____ SOLO level outcome because _____

_____

_____

My next step is to _____

_____

_____

Process maps to relate ideas (relational maps)

Here we focus on HookED maps and self-assessment rubrics to:

- Explain causes (Figures 3.18 and 3.19)
- Explain effects (Figures 3.20 and 3.21)
- Form an analogy (Figures 3.22 and 3.23).

Other resources for relating ideas are maps and self-assessment rubrics for:

- HOT SOLO Analyse (Hook and Mills 2011)
- HOT SOLO Classify (Hook and Mills 2011)
- HOT SOLO Compare and contrast (Hook and Mills 2011)
- HOT SOLO Sequence (Hook and Mills 2011).

Explain causes – Why did it happen? How did it happen?

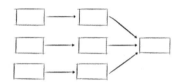

What are these resources for? You can use the HookED Explain causes map and self-assessment rubric to clarify the causes of an event or outcome.

How do I use them? Follow this step-by-step guide in which you lead students through the process of responding to the map before they try it for themselves, guided by the success criteria in the self-assessment rubric.

1. Align the HookED SOLO Explain causes map and self-assessment rubric with the identified learning intention. For example, "We are learning to explain the cause of [content] [context]."

2. Place the event in the Event box on the right-hand side of the map. It may be represented by text, a drawing, a photograph, a video, a graph or an extract from a newspaper.

3. List possible causes for the event in the boxes to the left of the Event box.

4. Place a speech bubble next to each cause and explain why it is a cause. For example, "This is a cause because ..."

5. Make a generalisation about the causes of the event. For example, "Overall I think ... because ... because ..."

6. Share with the students the success criteria for explaining causes in the HookED SOLO Explain causes self-assessment rubric.

7. With reference to the success criteria, students create their own causal explanation statement using relevant causes and the target vocabulary in the HookED SOLO Explain causes map. They may write or say these statements or convey them through an annotated drawing. This process is iterative, meaning that students can repeat it whenever new learning occurs and thus can improve on their original statement.

8. Students self- or peer-assess their causal explanations and seek teacher feedback on them.

9. Students assess their learning outcome for the identified learning intention against the SOLO levels, explain why they have chosen this level of learning outcome for their work (feedback) and suggest "where to next" steps (feed up).

10. Students record their work in a student learning log.

Figure 3.18: Template for HookED SOLO Explain causes map

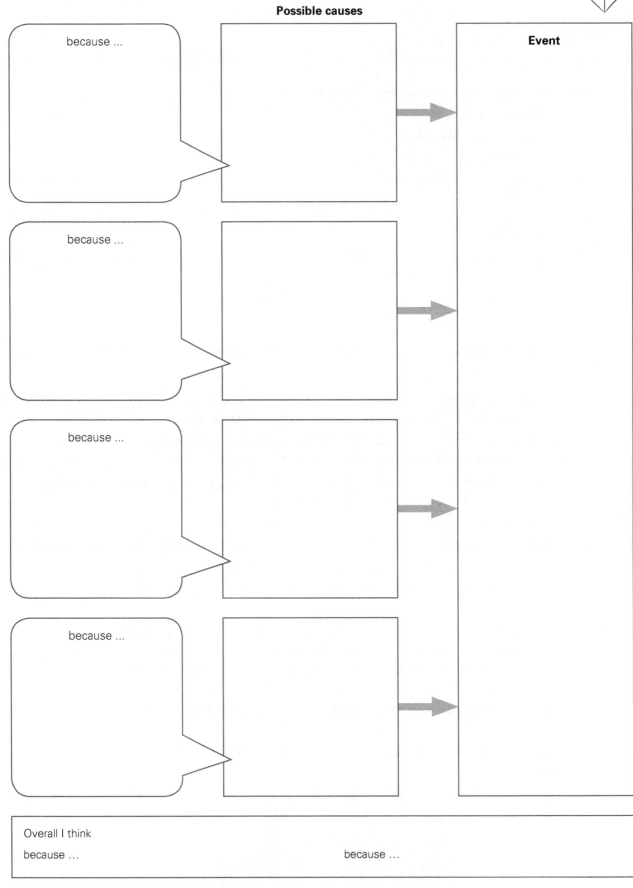

Possible causes

Event

because ...

because ...

because ...

because ...

Overall I think

because ...

because ...

SOLO level	Learning outcome	
Extended abstract 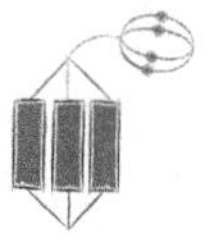	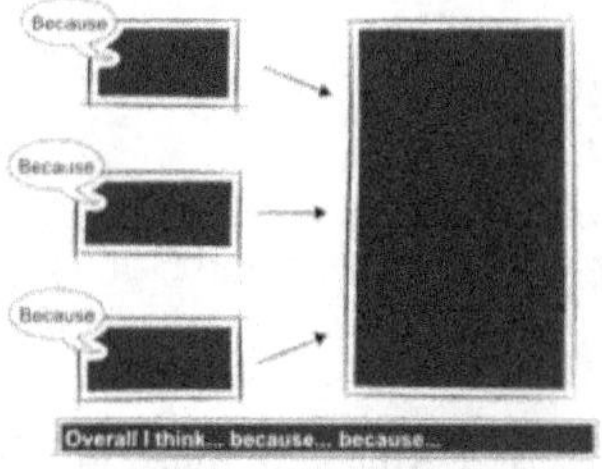	**... and** I look at it in a new way.
Relational 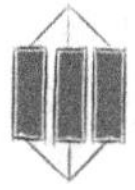	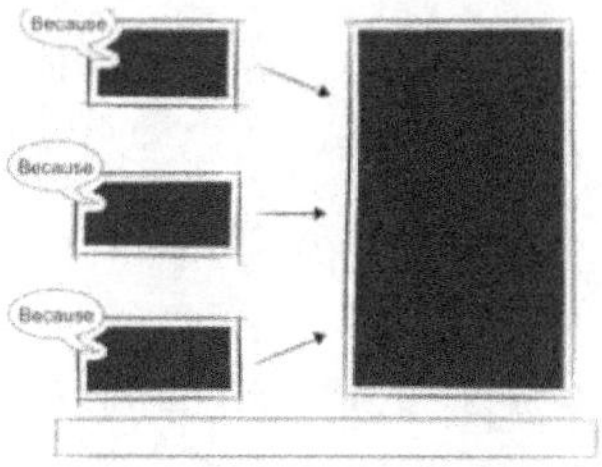	**and** I explain how the causes relate to the event ...
Multistructural 	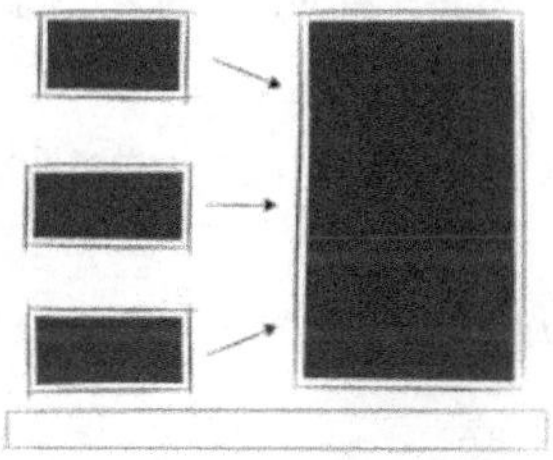	I identify the event and several relevant causes for the event ...
Unistructural 	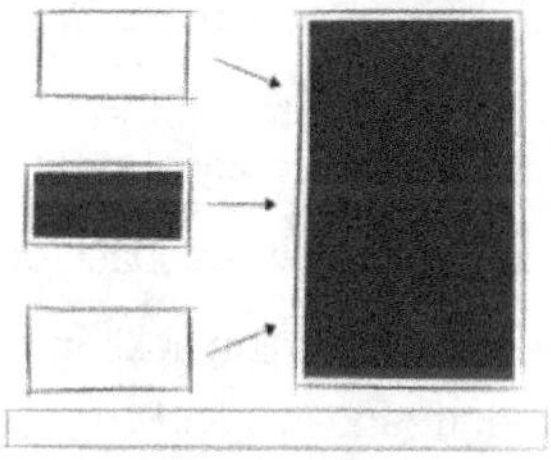	I identify the event and one relevant cause for the event.
Prestructural 	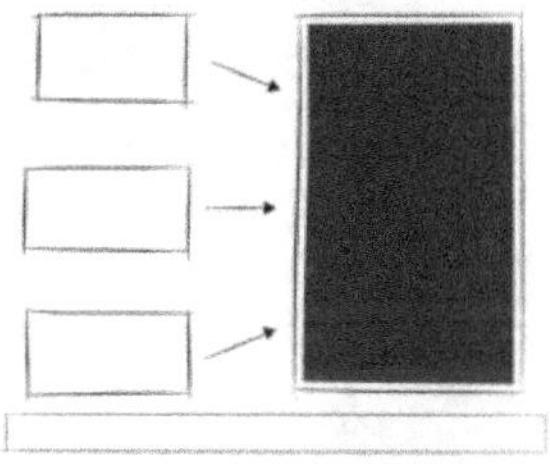	I identify the event but need help to identify the causes for the event.

My learning outcome is _____ because _____

_____

_____

My next step is to _____

_____

_____

Explain effects – What happened as a result? What was the consequence?

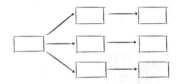

What are these resources for? You can use the HookED Explain effects map and self-assessment rubric to clarify the effects of an event or outcome.

How do I use them? Follow this step-by-step guide in which you lead students through the process of responding to the map before they try it for themselves, guided by the success criteria in the self-assessment rubric.

1. Align the HookED SOLO Explain effects map and self-assessment rubric with the identified learning intention. For example, "We are learning to explain the effect of [content] [context]."

2. Place the event in the Event box on the left-hand side of the map. It may be represented by text, a drawing, a photograph, a video, a graph or an extract from a newspaper.

3. List possible effects or consequences for the event in the boxes to the right of the Event box. Note students may create temporal sequence of short-term, medium-term and long-term effects.

4. Place a speech bubble next to each effect and explain why it is an effect. For example, "This is an effect because …"

5. Make a generalisation about the consequences or effects of the event. For example, "Overall I think … because … because …"

6. Share with the students the success criteria for explaining effects in the HookED SOLO Explain effects self-assessment rubric.

7. With reference to the success criteria, students create their own causal explanation statement using relevant effects and the target vocabulary from the HookED SOLO Explain effects map. They may write or say these statements or convey them through an annotated drawing. This process is iterative, meaning that students can repeat it whenever new learning occurs and thus can improve on their original statement.

8. Students self- or peer-assess their causal explanations and seek teacher feedback on them.

9. Students assess their learning outcome for the identified learning intention against the SOLO levels, explain why they have chosen this level of learning outcome for their work (feedback) and suggest "where to next" steps (feed up).

10. Students record their work in a student learning log.

Figure 3.20: Template for HookED SOLO Explain effects map

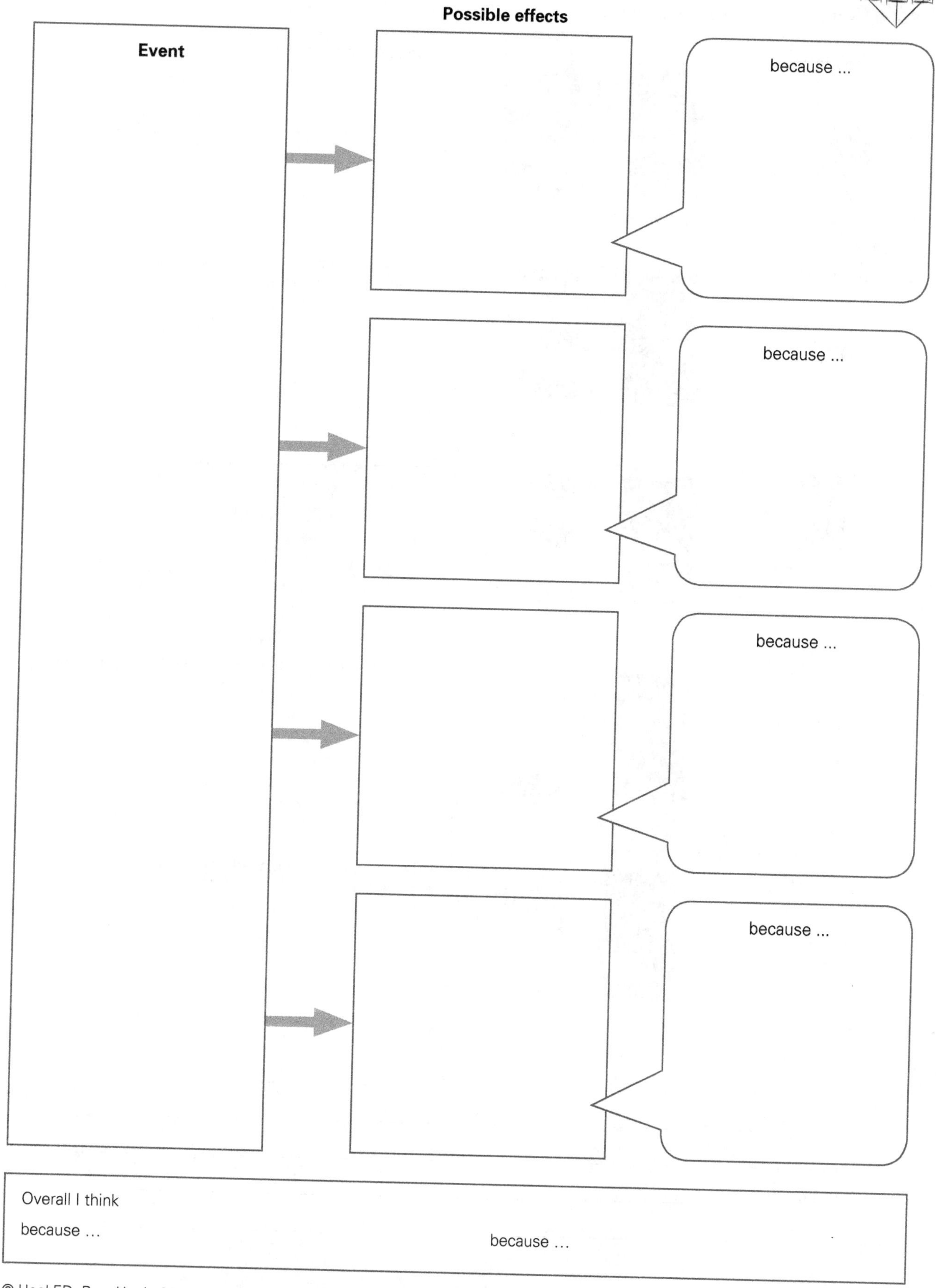

Possible effects

Event

because ...

because ...

because ...

because ...

Overall I think

because ...

because ...

Figure 3.21: Template for HookED SOLO Explain effects self-assessment rubric

SOLO level	Learning outcome	
Extended abstract 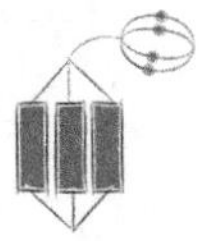	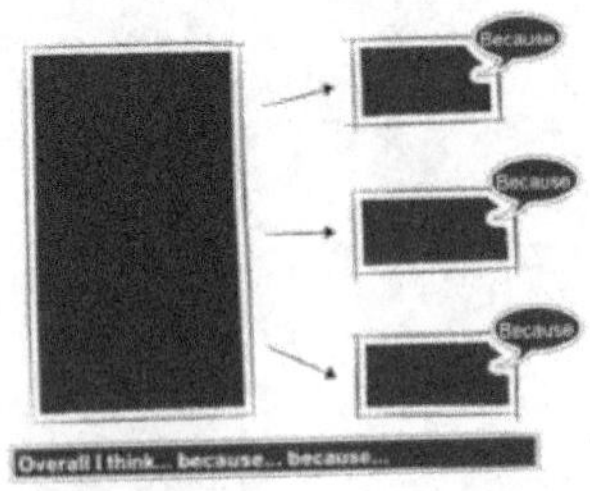	**... and** I look at the event in a new way.
Relational 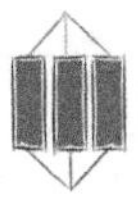	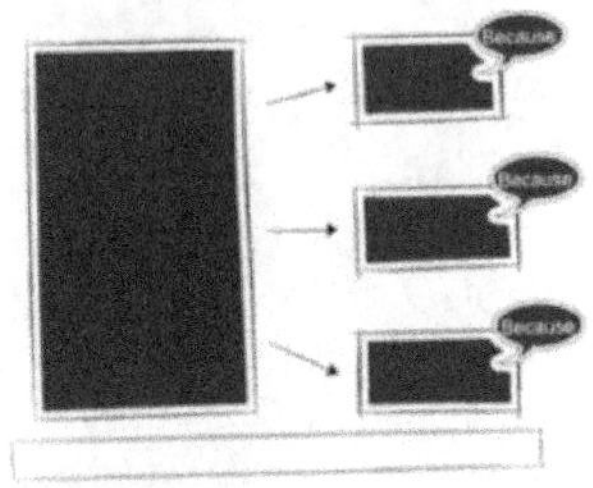	**... and** I explain how the effects (short-, medium- and long-term) relate to the event ...
Multistructural 	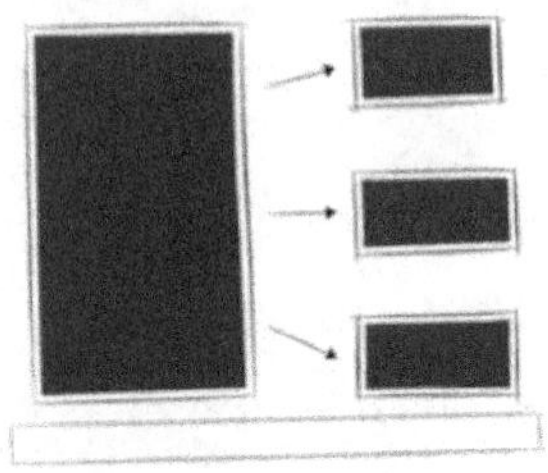	I identify the event and several relevant effects of the event ...
Unistructural 	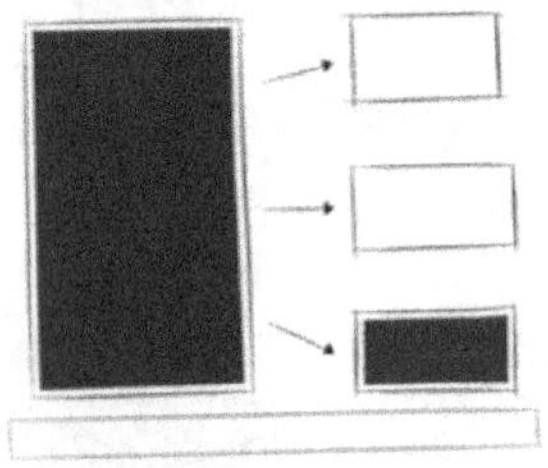	I identify the event and one relevant effect of the event.
Prestructural 	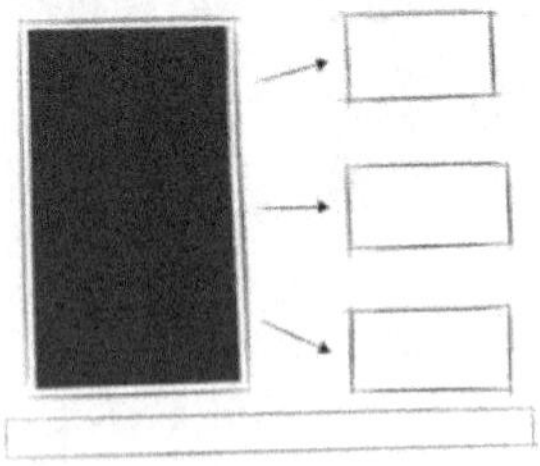	I identify the event but need help to identify the effects of the event.

My learning outcome is _____ because _____

_____

_____

My next step is to _____

_____

_____

Form an analogy – A is to B as C is to what?

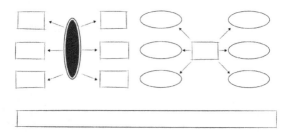

What are these resources for? You can use the HookED Form an analogy map and self-assessment rubric to find similarities between two objects that are not normally alike in structure.

How do I use these resources? Follow this step-by-step guide in which you lead students through the process of responding to the map before they try it for themselves, guided by the success criteria in the self-assessment rubric.

1. Align the HookED Form an analogy map and self-assessment rubric with the learning intention. For example, "We are learning to form an analogy for [content] [context]."

2. Choose an idea, activity or thing and place it in the centre of the first map in the upper half of the page.

3. Describe the features of the idea, activity or thing you wish to form an analogy for. Place these attributes in the boxes around the first map.

4. Choose one essential characteristic/attribute and place it in the centre of the second map in the bottom half of the page.

5. Use the second map to describe other ideas, activities or things that share the same characteristic. Think widely.

6. Choose an idea, activity or thing that captures your attention.

7. Use this to form an analogy with the first idea.

8. With reference to the success criteria, students create their own analogy using the content ideas in the HookED SOLO Form an analogy map. They may write or say these statements or convey them through an annotated drawing. This process is iterative, meaning that students can repeat it whenever new learning occurs and thus can improve on the original analogy.

9. Students self- or peer-assess their analogies and seek teacher feedback on them.

10. Students assess their learning outcome for the identified learning intention against the SOLO levels, explain why they have chosen this level of learning outcome for their work (feedback) and suggest "where to next" steps (feed up).

11. Students record their work in a student learning log.

Step 1: Describe the features of the idea, activity or thing you wish to make an analogy for.

Step 2: Choose one essential characteristic.

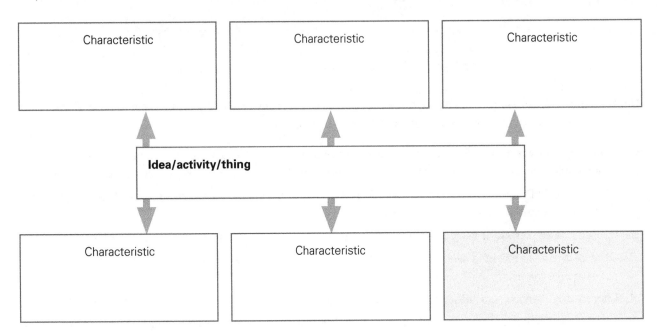

Step 3: Use the second map to describe other ideas, activities or things that share the same characteristic. Think widely.

Step 4: Choose an idea, activity or thing that captures your attention.

Step 5: Use this to form an analogy with the first idea in the box at the bottom of this page.

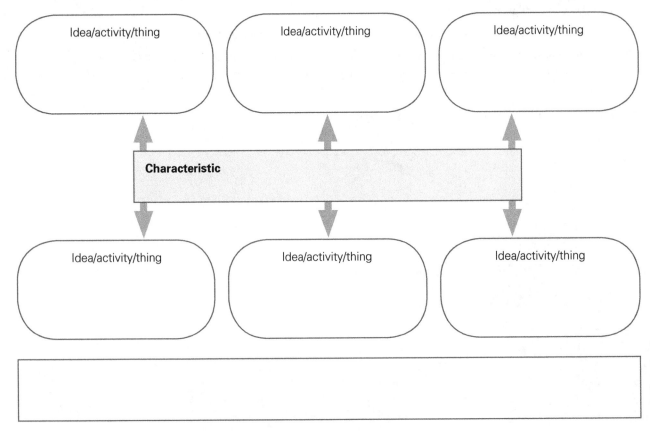

Figure 3.23: Template for HookED SOLO Form an analogy self-assessment rubric

SOLO level	Learning outcome	
Extended abstract 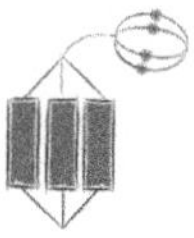	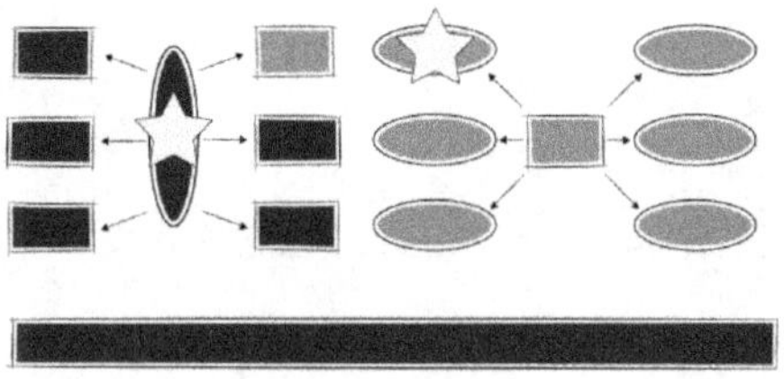	... **and** I can make an analogy.
Relational 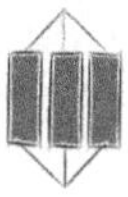	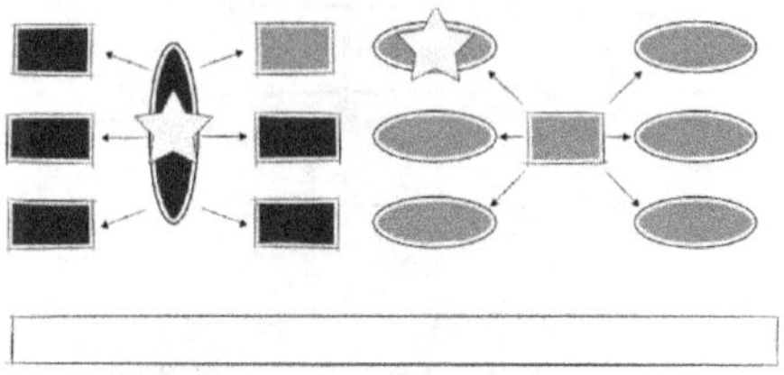	... **and** I can make a link between one of these attributes and my initial idea/activity/ thing ...
Multistructural 	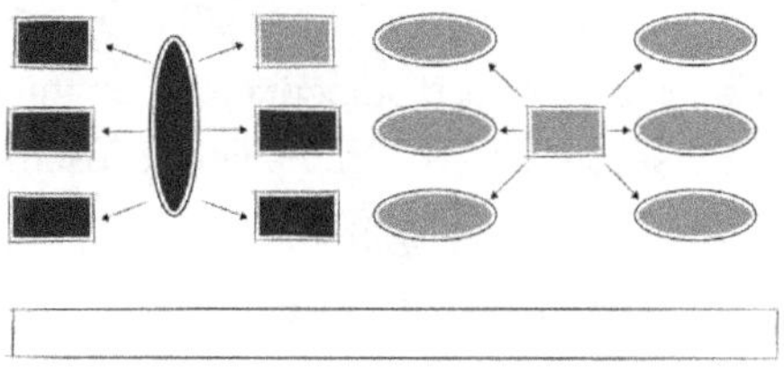	... **and** I can select one attribute and describe this again ...
Unistructural 	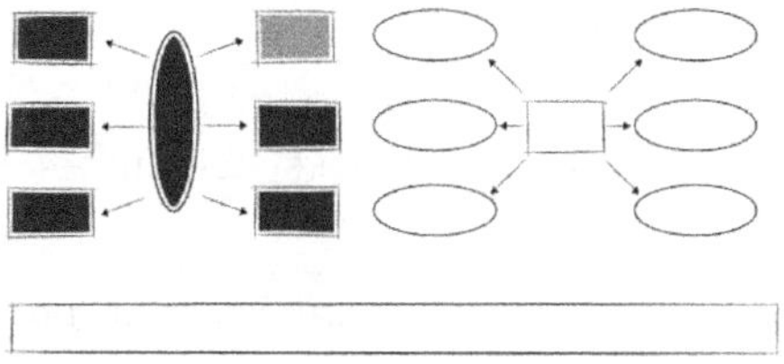	I can describe the essential attributes of the idea/activity/thing ...
Prestructural 	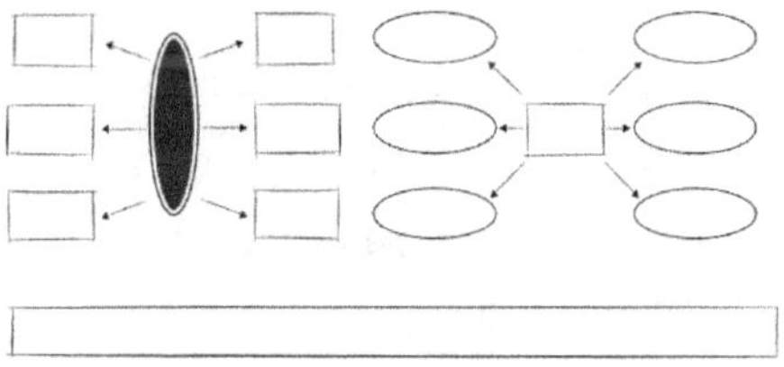	I can identify the idea/activity/thing.

My learning outcome is _____ because _____

_____

_____

My next step is to _____

_____

_____

Process maps to extend ideas (extended abstract maps)

Here we focus on the HOT SOLO Generalise map (Figure 3.24) and accompanying self-assessment rubric (Figure 3.25).

Other resources for extending ideas are the maps and self-assessment rubrics for:

- HOT SOLO Evaluate (Hook and Mills 2011)
- HOT SOLO Predict (Hook and Mills 2011).

Generalise – Overall I think … because … because …

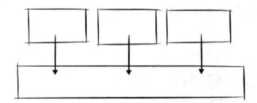

What are these resources for? You can use the HOT SOLO Generalise map and self-assessment rubric to back up the reliability and validity of a claim.

How do I use them? Follow this step-by-step guide in which you lead students through the process of responding to the map before they try it for themselves, guided by the success criteria in the self-assessment rubric.

1. Align the HOT SOLO Generalise map and self-assessment rubric with the identified learning intention. For example, "We are learning to make a generalisation about [content] [context]."

2. Make a generalisation/claim, or identify a claim in the editorial section of a local paper (print) or reader comments (online).

3. Clarify the meaning of the generalisation/claim.

4. Provide reasons to support the generalisation. For example, after the first "because …", explain why the claim is reliable.

5. Provide evidence/grounds to support your reasons. For example, after the second "because", explain why this reason is valid.

6. Evaluate the generalisation.

7. Share the success criteria for making a generalisation in the HOT SOLO Generalise self-assessment rubric.

8. With reference to the success criteria, students create their own generalisation statement using the completed HOT SOLO Generalise map. They may write or say the generalisation or convey it through an annotated drawing. This process is iterative, meaning that it can be repeated whenever new learning occurs and thus can improve on the original generalisation.

9. Students self- or peer-assess their generalisations and seek teacher feedback on them.

10. Students assess their learning outcome for the identified learning intention against the SOLO levels, explain why they have chosen this level of learning outcome for their work (feedback) and suggest "where to next" steps (feed up).

11. Students record their work in a student learning log.

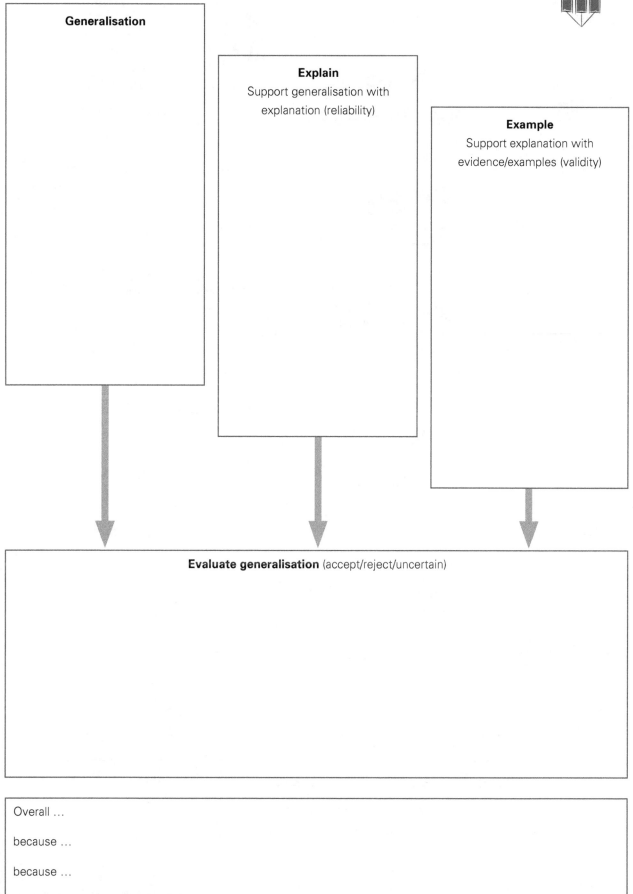

Generalisation

Explain
Support generalisation with explanation (reliability)

Example
Support explanation with evidence/examples (validity)

Evaluate generalisation (accept/reject/uncertain)

Overall …

because …

because …

Figure 3.25: Template for HOT SOLO Generalise self-assessment rubric

SOLO level	Learning outcome	
Extended abstract 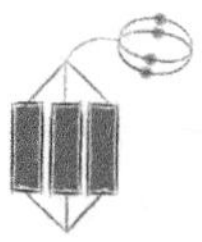	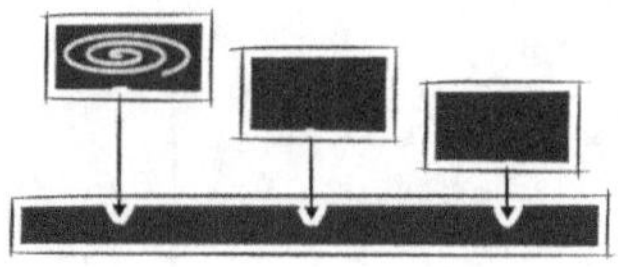	**... and** I can: • provide evidence to support it • evaluate the generalisation.
Relational 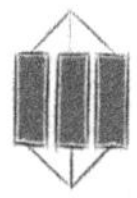	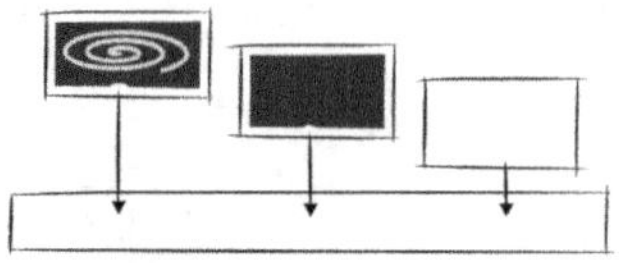	**... and** I can provide reasons to support it ...
Multistructural 	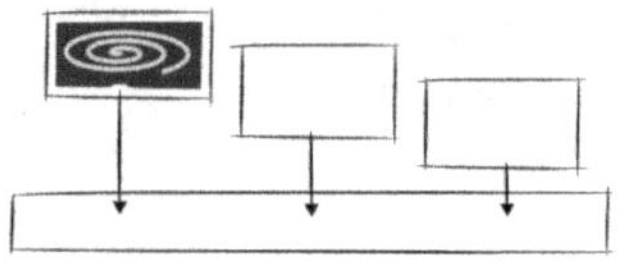	**... and** I can clarify its meaning ...
Unistructural 	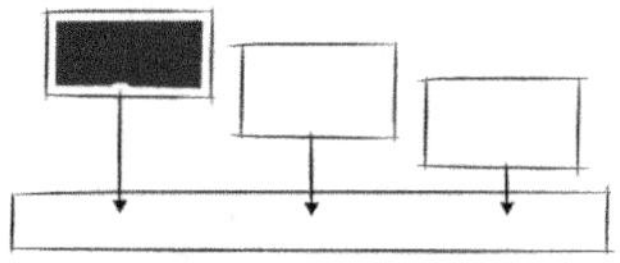	I can make a generalisation ...
Prestructural 	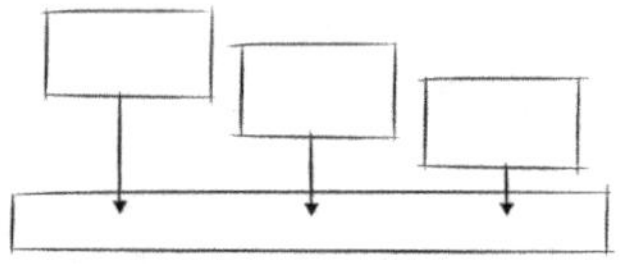	I need help to make a generalisation.

My generalisation is at a _____ SOLO level outcome because _____

_____

_____

My next step is to _____

_____

_____

Introducing SOLO in everyday acts of teaching

It is easy and productive to make SOLO Taxonomy part of everyday teaching activities – which may be anything from determining prior knowledge and setting learning intentions, to monitoring and assessment, to giving and receiving feedback – as we explore in the final pages of this section.

Determining prior knowledge

You can use SOLO to assess:

- the cognitive complexity of what students know about and can do before starting – to determine their prior knowledge and understanding
- students' prior skills and even their disposition towards learning (see Table 3.1 on the next page).

Finding out what students already know (declarative knowledge) and can do (functioning knowledge) is important if we are to plan teaching and learning activities that will enable all students to achieve the targeted outcome. If we teach what students already understand and/or what is beyond their immediate grasp, we risk disengaging them from learning because they are waiting to learn something new or to find something they can relate to.

Declarative knowledge: One approach is to set up prior knowledge tasks and use SOLO to determine the level of complexity of understanding shown in the students' responses. These tasks can vary widely – from undertaking a SOLO hexagon activity, to drawing a picture or responding to a quiz with questions set at different SOLO levels, to responding to a series of open-ended questions differentiated by SOLO level.

For example, before studying the rise in popularity of teenage fiction (text and film) featuring dystopian future worlds, you might run a SOLO hexagon activity in which students:

- record what they already know about dystopian fiction on the hexagons
- look for opportunities to connect ideas
- annotate the connections
- step back and make an overall claim.

Alternatively you might ask students to respond to questions formulated at different levels of cognitive complexity:

▥▥▥ **Describe** a character, setting or plot commonly found in texts (books and film) featuring dystopian futures (multistructural task).

▥▥▥ **Explain** how or why this character, setting or plot is typical of dystopian-themed texts (relational task).

▥▥▥ **Discuss** the present-day implications of this character, setting or plot for how we choose to act as citizens (extended abstract task).

You can also ask students to self- and/or peer-assess their level of prior knowledge: do they have no idea about novels about dystopian future worlds, one idea, many ideas, related ideas or extended ideas? Students can share the level they identify using symbols, words or hand signs.

Functioning knowledge: In a similar way you can set prior knowledge assessment tasks to determine the students' SOLO level of functioning knowledge. Table 3.1 sets out an example of a SOLO functioning knowledge rubric for demonstrating self-efficacy when learning.

To assess prior knowledge, you may observe students as they perform a task. Alternatively both you and your students may undertake a series of observations, with students assessing both themselves (eg, through video recording) and their peers.

These observations help determine whether a student's performance:

- showed they had no idea as to how to approach the task
- was prompted or directed
- was independent but involved errors because the student was not sure about the purpose of their actions
- was independent, strategic or purposeful and self-correcting
- was independent and extended the student in new ways.

You and your students can share these outcomes using symbols, words or hand signs.

Table 3.1: SOLO self-assessment rubric for demonstrating self-efficacy

	Prestructural	Unistructural	Multistructural	Relational	Extended abstract
Functioning knowledge					
	[needs help]	[if directed]	[aware but no reasons, has a go, makes mistakes]	[purposeful, strategic, knows why and when, can identify mistakes]	[new ways, seeks feedback to improve, acts as role model, teaches others]
Learning intention *demonstrate* [verb] *self-efficacy* [context] *when learning* [context]	I need help to start.	I take on difficult tasks if directed or shown exactly what to do.	I take on difficult tasks but I look for opportunities to give up and stop when I make mistakes or it gets too hard.	I take on difficult tasks. I enjoy the challenges they present. I see challenges as a chance to learn more and make a greater effort. I find and correct my own mistakes …	… **and** I seek feedback to improve what I am doing. I help others. I am a role model for others. I find new ways of doing the challenge.

Clarifying learning intentions (desired learning outcomes)

Learning intentions describe what we want students to learn. Making learning intentions and success criteria visible is an important part of any successful experience of teaching and learning (see Black and Wiliam 1998a, 1998b).

Learning intentions focus on the knowledge, skills, attitudes and behaviours identified in the relevant curriculum documents. We can zoom out and consider the big-picture goals of the curriculum learning areas, key competencies and values, or zoom in on achievement objectives and/or some explicit sub-goal within the achievement objective that forms the basis for a unit or lesson plan.

When making learning intentions visible to students, it is important to determine the **kind of knowledge** that students need to understand and **the level of understanding** they need to achieve. Regardless of whether the learning intention is focused on declarative or functioning knowledge, to make the learning visible to students we can clarify the learning intention by sharing the SOLO level of the intended learning outcome. For example, "This learning intention sits at the relational level because it is asking you to connect ideas by explaining them."

To specify a SOLO level for a learning outcome, we need to think about the purpose of the knowledge we are teaching. For example, if students are learning about:

- "the impact of lowering the driving speed limits on our society", we are determining the influence of a lower speed limit on our lives – an extended abstract task
- "the driving speed limits", then we are describing the speed limits – a multistructural task
- "the similarities and differences between the speed limits in our country and Germany", then we are comparing and contrasting – a relational task.

Aligning verbs with SOLO levels. Verbs are aligned with the different SOLO levels (Biggs and Collis 1982) according to their purpose. For example:

- *define* and *describe* prompt students to bring in ideas – unistructural and multistructural outcomes
- *compare* and *contrast*, *analyse* and *explain* prompt for linking ideas – relational outcomes
- *evaluate* and *reflect* prompt students to extend their thinking to new contexts – extended abstract outcomes.

Table 3.2 offers a longer list of verbs aligned with each SOLO learning outcome.

Inform students of the SOLO level of the verb in a learning intention by positioning a SOLO symbol alongside the learning intention on the whiteboard and/or by hand signing the level.

Table 3.2: Verbs aligned against SOLO learning outcomes

Unistructural	Multistructural	Relational	Extended abstract
Verbs for bringing in ideas		Verbs for connecting ideas	Verbs for extending ideas
Define	Describe	Formulate questions	Evaluate
Identify	List	Compare and contrast	Theorise
Name	Combine	Explain causes	Generalise
Label	Follow algorithm	Explain effects	Predict
Do a simple procedure	Outline	Sequence	Create
Memorise	Separate	Classify	Imagine
Recognise		Analyse (part–whole)	Hypothesise
Count		Relate	Reflect
Draw		Form an analogy	Compose
Find		Apply	Invent
Label		Integrate	Prove from first principles
Match		Argue	Make an original case
Quote		Organise	
Recall			
Recite			
Imitate			

Source: Biggs and Tang (2007) and Hook and Mills (2011)

Tip: The SOLO level of a verb can vary

Biggs notes that the alignment of a verb with a SOLO level can vary according to the nature of the task, so be prepared to be flexible when necessary. For example, Biggs and Tang (2007, p 80) show *classify* and *sequence* as multistructural verbs but I have found it more useful to align these two verbs with relational tasks and linking ideas in the learning contexts of primary and secondary classrooms (Hook and Mills 2011, p 13).

Aligning learning intentions with the learning goal (constructive alignment)

Constructive alignment is a principle for aligning what needs to be learnt (curriculum goals), what the students will do (learning intentions), the learning experiences provided to meet the learning intention and how the learning outcomes from these experiences will be assessed or demonstrated (success criteria) (Figure 3.26) (Biggs 1999; Biggs and Tang 2007).

Figure 3.26: Aspects of learning targeted for constructive alignment

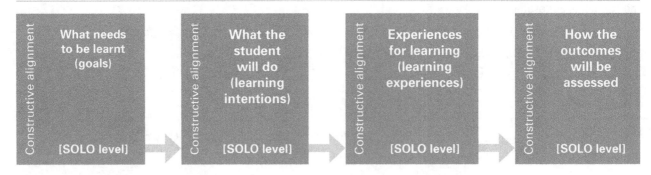

When designing learning intentions or a learning goal, it is important to move beyond the broad-brush verbs commonly used in learning goals like "understand" or "be aware of". As Biggs and Tang (1979, p 74) point out, it is far from clear what such words mean to teachers, let alone to students. When goals are not pinned down, it is impossible to reliably determine if and when students reach them and they are less likely to be visible to students.

To share learning goals in ways that are meaningful to students, we must use more nuanced learning verbs. We can set a series of explicit, proximate and hierarchical learning intentions by using nuanced verbs at different levels of SOLO along with the content and any context the verb is designed to address:

> Learning intention: [insert verb] [insert content] [insert context]. – SOLO level of task

Each learning intention should prepare students for the next one, so that you have a scaffolded list of learning intentions that build understanding towards the overall learning goal. You can then use these SOLO-differentiated learning intentions to develop SOLO-differentiated learning experiences.

For example, if your desired goal is that students **understand the impact** of cage diving on shark behaviour off Stewart Island in New Zealand, then the desired learning goal might be expressed as:

> [**verb:** Explain the effect] of [**content:** cage diving operations] [**context:** on the behaviour of great white sharks off Stewart Island].

The scaffolded list of possible learning intentions might include the following:

Define great white shark. (Unistructural)

Define cage diving. (Unistructural)

Describe cage diving off Stewart Island. (Multistructural)

Describe the behaviour of great white sharks off Stewart Island before cage diving was introduced. (Multistructural)

Describe the behaviour of great white sharks off Stewart Island after cage diving was introduced. (Multistructural)

Compare and contrast the behaviour of great white sharks off Stewart Island before and after cage diving was introduced. (Relational).

Make a generalisation about the impact of cage diving on the behaviour of great white sharks off Stewart Island. (Extended abstract)

Evaluate the claim that cage diving is changing the behaviour of great white sharks off Stewart Island. (Extended abstract)

In a similar way, as Table 3.3 shows, you can clarify the New Zealand Curriculum's broad achievement objectives for teachers and students by expressing them as differentiated learning intentions or intended learning outcomes using SOLO verbs.

Students can also use this process of differentiating learning intentions when planning their own research or student inquiry.

Table 3.3: Alignment of achievement objectives with learning outcomes in the New Zealand Curriculum

Achievement objective	Intended learning outcomes
Level Three: Social Studies Students will gain knowledge, skills and experience to: **understand** how cultural practices vary but reflect similar purposes.	**Define** culture. (Unistructural) **Define** cultural practice. (Unistructural) **List** cultures. (Multistructural) **List** cultural practices. (Multistructural) **Describe** one or more cultural practices. (Multistructural) **Explain** the purpose for a cultural practice. (Relational) **Compare and contrast** cultural practices. (Relational) **Classify** cultural practices according to their purpose. (Relational) **Make a generalisation** about cultural practices. (Extended abstract) **Reflect** on the similarities in purpose between your own cultural practice and the practices of other cultures. (Extended abstract)

Effective strategies for student progress

Strategically selected interventions support students in their learning as they progress across each level of SOLO.

Teachers already have a range of strategies and interventions they use to help students learn. Asking them to throw these out and start using a strategy branded as a "SOLO strategy" would be futile and completely unnecessary. A more productive approach is to engage teachers in coding the strategies they already use on the basis of which SOLO level of learning outcome each of those strategies supports.

When students can access a differentiated toolbox of effective strategies for learning, we add choice and challenge to their learning. In addition, a SOLO toolbox of strategies supports the learning needs of diverse students, allowing teachers and students to identify cognitively appropriate learning interventions in thinking and e-learning (Hook 2012).

Tip: SOLO toolbox of effective strategies

Create a framework for a SOLO toolbox of strategies on a classroom wall. Encourage students to add effective strategies to it as they come across them over the year.

Alternatively create an online SOLO toolbox, using an application such as Pinterest to host strategies for multistructural, relational and extended abstract thinking.

Monitoring and assessing learning progress

As a model for assessing the complexity of learning outcomes and the learning process, SOLO is used to:

- determine prior knowledge
- develop differentiated assessment items in tests[1]
- develop success criteria for learning intentions or achievement objectives.

When using SOLO rubrics to monitor and assess learning progress, you can greatly enhance students' progress across each SOLO level by including them in the discussion of effective strategies.

For example, the following rubrics identify effective strategies for giving feedback (Table 3.4) and developing respect for others (Table 3.5).

---

1   For example, e-asTTle is an online assessment tool developed to assess students' achievement and progress in reading, mathematics and writing, and in pānui, pāngarau and tuhituhi. It uses SOLO Taxonomy to design test items to determine the cognitive complexity of the assessment tasks and responses (http://e-asttle.tki.org.nz).

Table 3.4: Star and a wish feedback rubric

Functioning knowledge	●	▌	▐▐▐	▐▐▐	▐▐▐
I am learning to give kind and helpful feedback to others.	I need help to give feedback.	I can look at another learner's work.	I can give feedback (a star) about another learner's work.	I can give feedback (a star) that connects to the learning goal (wish).	I can give feedback (a star) that connects to the learning goal and I suggest a next step (wish).
Effective strategies from the learners	I might say, "I finished my work." I just think about my work.	I might say, "I'll look at your work." I might just say, "That's beautiful."	I might say, "I like how you …"	I might ask, "What was your goal?" Then I might say, "I like how you …"	I might say, "I like how you … and then you could …"
I am learning to ask for and listen to feedback from others.	I do my work.	I ask another learner for feedback.	I can listen to the feedback from another learner. I can tell someone what they said.	I notice if the feedback connects to my goal.	I listen to the feedback and make a choice about my next step.
Effective strategies co-constructed with learners	I might say, "I finished." I just think about my work.	I might say, "Please can you look at my work? Can you please give me feedback? Can you please give me a star and a wish?"	I look at the person talking. I might tell my teacher, "Jack told me he liked how I …".	I might think, "My learning goal was … This feedback is helpful because …"	I might choose to make a change or ignore the feedback.

Source: Bridget Cassé, Edendale School, Auckland, New Zealand

Table 3.5: SOLO self-assessment rubric for respecting the rights and feelings of others

Functioning knowledge	●	❘	❘❘❘	◈❘❘❘	◈❘❘❘⊶
I can demonstrate respect for the rights and feelings of others. • Show self-control. • Include everyone. • Solve conflicts peacefully. • Do not disrupt the work and play of others.	I need help to know what showing self-control looks like. *It is not my problem. Everyone for themselves – dog eat dog kind of world. If I didn't do it, someone else would have.*	I can show self-control if I am directed. *I can care for others if I am directed or reminded.*	I use several strategies to help me demonstrate self-control but I am not sure how, when and/or why to use them. *(Trial and error; aware of strategies but not sure why or when to use them so makes mistakes)* *I can give it a go but I sometimes forget and rely on others.*	I use several strategies to show self-control and I know how, when and why to use them … *(Strategic or purposeful use of strategies; knows why and when)* *I am on to it. I keep an eye out for others and explain why or justify.*	… **and** I can encourage others to show self-control. I act as a role model for others to help them show self-control. *I extend this to contexts outside of school. It has become part of who I am; habitual.* *I get irritated if I am prevented from acting in this way.*
Effective strategies *[insert strategies suggested by students and teachers]*	Show examples. Give opportunity to practise.	Give external feedback Give clear instructions (step by step). Prompt. Do situational teaching.	Revisit, recap and remind. Conduct autopsies or debrief. Do role plays. Shift to internal feedback.	Give repeated opportunities to practise.	

Source: Based on Hellison's Model of Social Responsibility: Level One (Year 12)

As noted in Section 2, a key advantage of using SOLO is that the task and the learning outcome can be at different levels. So students can monitor their progress when using any learning verb using SOLO-differentiated success criteria for the outcome of the task and effective strategies to progress each level (Hook and Mills 2011, 2012).

> **Tip: Resources for monitoring and assessing learning progress**
> * HOT and HookED SOLO visual process maps and self-assessment rubrics that students can use to draft their written or oral responses for verbs at different levels: see page 43
> * SOLO visual success criteria: http://pamhook.com/tools/SelfAssessment.html#slide0
> * SOLO Declarative Knowledge Rubric Generator (Figure 3.27): http://pamhook.com/solo-apps/declarative-knowledge-rubric-generator
> * SOLO Functioning Knowledge Rubric Generator (Figure 3.28): http://pamhook.com/solo-apps/functioning-knowledge-rubric-generator

Giving and receiving feedback

When teachers use SOLO with students, they notice both students and teachers give, receive and discuss feedback more effectively. Both teachers and students use SOLO levels as a common language for describing the depth of learning in student outcomes. These feedback conversations may be between students, between students and teachers, or between teachers.

Supported by the SOLO-differentiated nature of these tasks, assessment criteria and feedback, students learn to think in a richly metacognitive way about the learning task. They use SOLO levels to:

- give and receive feedback on the cognitive complexity of the learning task (what am I doing?)

- monitor how well they are doing the task (how is it going?)

- make informed decisions about their next steps (what should I do next?).

By using SOLO in this way, students can give their teachers explicit feedback on the depth of their understanding and the help they will need for achieving their next steps. Teachers can respond in a similar manner. The nuanced feedback helps reinforce students' understanding that their learning outcomes are due to their efforts and effective strategies rather than luck or fixed ability.

> **Tip: Encourage metacognitive thinking**
>
> Co-construct SOLO rubrics (success criteria) with students and encourage them to suggest "+ 1" strategies for progressing their learning to the next SOLO level. These are powerful ways of building their fluency in using SOLO as a model for metacognitive reflection.

Figure 3.27: SOLO Declarative Knowledge Rubric Generator   **Figure 3.28: SOLO Functioning Knowledge Rubric Generator**

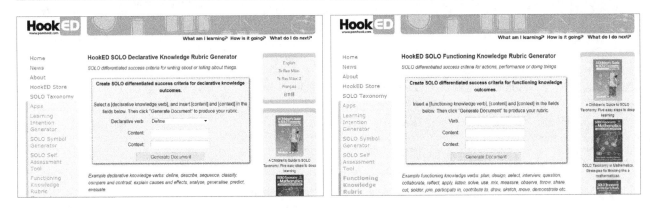

Zooming out

You can use SOLO to:

- design differentiated learning tasks to challenge students to develop surface, deep and conceptual understanding

- develop differentiated success criteria to clarify assessment outcomes for declarative and functioning knowledge

- provide explicit feedback and feed-forward on next steps.

The next step is when students realise that a SOLO-level response in one developmental stage or task can become a response at a different level of outcome for a task at a higher level. Table 3.6 sets out an example in which:

- a student's learning outcome for a description (multistructural) task is at a relational level when describing the role of a sharemilker on a dairy farm because they have linked ideas by noting a difference between the levels of responsibility of a sharemilker and a farm owner

- the student zooms out to compare and contrast the role of a sharemilker with that of a farm owner – a relational task

- the student's identification of one similarity or difference between a sharemilker and a farm manager represents a unistructural learning outcome.

The SOLO "zoom out" effect means that when teachers design learning experiences for increasing cognitive complexity, there is no upper limit or boundary. From a student's perspective, there is no "sprint to the finish line" – there is always another step to increase the complexity of their learning outcome.

Table 3.6: Example of the SOLO "zoom out" effect

Multistructural task:			Zoom out to a relational task:	
Describe the role of a sharemilker on a dairy farm		**Student response**	Compare and contrast the role of a sharemilker with that of a farm owner	
Relational	My description has several relevant attributes and I make links.	A sharemilker feeds, moves and milks dairy cows on farms. They own a herd and work to produce as much high-quality milk as possible. They share their herd in exchange for a share of the milk company payouts. They differ from farm managers in the degree of their financial responsibilities because they are responsible for their herd while a farm manager is responsible for the farm finances and performance of the whole farm.	I can identify one relevant similarity or difference.	**Unistructural**

Tip: Aim beyond infinity

Use the SOLO "zoom out" effect to encourage students to adopt an attitude to learning akin to Buzz Lightyear's cry of "To infinity and beyond!" (*Toy Story*). This attitude has many advantages over a "check box – done that" approach, in which students see learning tasks as something to be ticked off and not revisited.

Conclusion

SOLO is a powerful model of learning that makes the structure of a learning outcome visible. In doing so, it provides a simple, reliable and systematically hierarchical way of describing how a student's learning outcome changes when mastering a learning goal. Both teachers and students use the model to reduce the gap between a student's current understandings or performance and the desired goal. It helps answer the important goal-focused questions:

- Where am I going?
- How am I going?
- Where to next?

The classroom-based approach of explicitly sharing SOLO with students, as described in this book, supports students in developing metacognition, self-regulation, self-efficacy, engagement and resilience when learning.

SOLO encourages students to create their own understanding of the world. The biggest problem in implementation is a failure to share the model with students so that it does not become their model of learning. The first steps described in the book will help teachers **and** students clarify surface and deep understanding and the learning process.

When we share SOLO with students, they tackle learning tasks with greater confidence and motivation for learning. They start to care about what they are learning and how they might use this new understanding to improve their own learning outcomes and from there to benefit others through deliberate acts of citizenship (Hook 2012).

Clearly, then, there are many powerful reasons why you and your students would benefit from SOLO Taxonomy. This book has also pointed out some easy and effective first steps for making it part of teaching and learning in your classroom. Why wait any longer?

References

Biggs, JB. (1999). *Teaching for Quality Learning at University*. Buckingham: Buckingham Open University Press.

Biggs, JB. (2013). *Changing Universities: A memoir about academe in different places and times*. Australia: Strictly Literary.

Biggs, JB and Collis, KF. (1982). *Evaluating the Quality of Learning: The SOLO Taxonomy*. New York: Academic Press.

Biggs, J and Tang, C. (2007). *Teaching for Quality Learning at University: What the student does* (3rd ed). Berkshire: Society for Research into Higher Education & Open University Press.

Black, P and Wiliam, D. (1998a). Assessment and classroom learning. *Assessment in Education* 5(1): 7–74.

Black, P and Wiliam, D. (1998b). *Inside the Black Box: Raising standards through classroom assessment*. London: King's College School of Education.

Blackwell, L, Trzesniewski, K and Dweck, CS. (2007). Implicit theories of intelligence predict achievement across an adolescent transition: A longitudinal study and an intervention. *Child Development* 78: 246–263.

Buckner, S. (2004). Empowering students from thinking to writing. In D Hyerle, S Curtis and L Alper (Eds) *Student Successes with Thinking Maps: School based research, results and models for achievement using visual tools* (pp 75–86). California: Corwin Press.

Cimpian, A, Arce, H, Markman, EM and Dweck, CS. (2007). Subtle linguistic cues impact children's motivation. *Psychological Science* 18: 314–316.

Dweck, CS. (1999). *Self-theories: Their role in motivation, personality and development*. Philadelphia: Taylor and Francis Psychology Press.

Dweck, CS. (2006). *Mindset: The new psychology of success*. New York: Random House.

Grant, H and Dweck, CS. (2003). Clarifying achievement goals and their impact. *Journal of Personality and Social Psychology* 85: 541–553.

Hattie, JAC. (2012). *Visible Learning for Teachers: Maximising impact on learning*. London: Routledge.

Hattie, JAC and Brown, GTL. (2004). *Cognitive Processes in asTTle: The SOLO Taxonomy*. asTTle Technical Report 43. University of Auckland/Ministry of Education.

Hodgson, AM. (1992). Hexagons for systems thinking. *European Journal of Systems Dynamics* 59(1): 220–230.

Hook, P. (2012). Teaching and learning: Tales from the ampersand. In L Rowan and C Bigum (Eds) *Future Proofing Education: Transformative approaches to new technologies and student diversity in futures oriented classrooms*. Netherlands: Springer.

Hook, P. (2013). *A Children's Guide to SOLO Taxonomy: Five easy steps to deep learning*. Invercargill: Essential Resources.

Hook, P and Cassé, B. (2013). *SOLO Taxonomy in the Early Years: Making connections for belonging, being and becoming*. Invercargill: Essential Resources.

Hook, P and Mills, J. (2011). *SOLO Taxonomy: A guide for schools. Book 1: A common language of learning*. Invercargill: Essential Resources.

Hook, P and Mills, J. (2012). *SOLO Taxonomy: A guide for schools. Book 2. Planning for differentiation*. Invercargill: Essential Resources.

Hook, P, Garrett, C, Howard, M and John, E. (2014). *SOLO Taxonomy in Mathematics: Strategies for thinking like a mathematician*. Invercargill: Essential Resources.

Kamins, M and Dweck, CS. (1999). Person vs process praise and criticism: Implications for contingent self-worth and coping. *Developmental Psychology* 35: 835–847.

Mangels, JA, Butterfield, B, Lamb, J, Good, CD and Dweck, CS. (2006). Why do beliefs about intelligence influence learning success? A social-cognitive-neuroscience model. *Social, Cognitive, and Affective Neuroscience* 1: 75–86.

McNeill, L and Hook, P. (2012). *SOLO Taxonomy and Making Meaning. Book 1: Text purposes, audiences and ideas*. Invercargill: Essential Resources.

Mueller, CM and Dweck, CS. (1998). Praise for intelligence can undermine children's motivation and performance. *Journal of Personality and Social Psychology* 75: 33–52.

Novak, JD. (2013). Concept mapping. In J Hattie and EM Anderman (Eds) *International Guide to Student Achievement* (pp 363–365). New York: Routledge.

Nussbaum, AD and Dweck, CS. (2008). Defensiveness vs remediation: Self-theories and modes of self-esteem maintenance. *Personality and Social Psychology Bulletin* 34(5): 599–612.

Silver, D. (2011). Using the 'Zone' to help reach every learner. *Kappa Delta Pi Record* 47(suppl 1): 28–31.

Smith, A and Turner, J. (Undated). Step Up. URL: www.alistairsmithlearning.com

Vygotsky, LS. (1978). *Mind in Society: The development of higher psychological processes*. Cambridge, MA: Harvard University Press.

Index of tables and figures

Tables

Figures

CPSIA information can be obtained
at www.ICGtesting.com
Printed in the USA
BVHW011351180819
555966BV00015B/228/P